Contents

1 Numbers

1.1 Arranging numbers

Mystic Meg attempts to predict the numbers in the Lottery. She sees the people who will be celebrating – perhaps!

- *What are your lucky numbers?*
- *How would you spend a Lottery jackpot?*

After every Lottery draw, the numbers are rearranged so that the smallest number is first. Then the numbers get bigger and bigger. This is called **ascending** order. This makes it easier to check your ticket.

Sort these numbers into ascending order. Put the smallest number first, then the next smallest, and so on.

❶ 21 37 14 82 93 57 8 42 51 12
❷ 81 72 53 91 17 9 31 46 39 75
❸ 15 63 45 28 6 37 65 84 90 21
❹ 53 50 72 41 48 63 27 13 91 38
❺ 5 17 80 32 12 3 61 45 55 72

❻ 67 33 52 16 27 98 73 57 11 9
❼ 40 27 19 72 58 65 61 71 32 26
❽ 19 35 6 84 70 23 14 8 26 91
❾ 36 20 15 10 29 3 62 71 19 53
❿ 83 62 15 74 89 75 91 30 59 68

Counting down

The countdown for a rocket launch is in **descending** order. It starts with the biggest number and ends with zero.

Sort these numbers into descending order. Put the largest number first.

❶ 14 28 61 7 19 32 47 80 29 33
❷ 60 43 17 82 90 75 70 16 58 113
❸ 38 71 52 81 39 41 57 62 19 7
❹ 58 74 16 18 50 65 70 39 48 75
❺ 61 85 36 55 70 12 6 10 74 93

❻ 64 70 93 21 54 75 87 99 31 77
❼ 58 7 16 25 76 69 92 37 54 32
❽ 81 95 27 48 98 85 62 71 87 90
❾ 45 37 25 42 81 39 48 67 43 75
❿ 18 54 30 12 71 60 38 72 91 28

Maths Plus

Pupil's Book 1

Published by Collins Educational
An imprint of HarperCollins*Publishers*
77–85 Fulham Palace Road,
London W6 8JB

© HarperCollins*Publishers* Ltd 1997

First published 1997

ISBN 000 322484 8

The Maths Plus writing team
Sheila Beniston
Paul Cherry
Elizabeth Forth
Jill Lane
Gareth Price

Designed by Chi Leung

Picture research by Caroline Thompson

Artwork by Barking Dog Art

Printed in Great Britain by
Bath Press Colourbooks, Glasgow

Repro by Applescan Reproductions plc

Acknowledgements

Every effort has been made to contact the holders of copyright material, but if any have been inadvertently overlooked, the publishers will be pleased to make the necessary arrangements at the first opportunity.

Photographs
The publishers would like to thank the following for permission to reproduce photographs:
(T = top, B = bottom, C = centre, L = left, R = right)

Allsport 44, 68, Allsport/A Want 14, J Gichigi 15, P Cole 20, D Cannon 26, Vandystadt 60BR; BBC Stills Library 4, 77, BBC/ICM/Amanda Howard Associates 41; Kathy Braund 30; The Old Bushmills Distillery Co Ltd 58; Bruce Coleman Ltd: G Cozzi 56, J McDonald 75, J Grayson 61BL; Brian Shuel/Collections 72; Ford Motor Company Ltd 69; Getty Images 6, 10, 37, 38B, 40, 42, 45, 60TR, 61TR, 70; Ronald Grant Archive 16, 64; Photographer: Mike Vaughan © Grant Naylor Productions Ltd 48; Sally and Richard Greenhill 38T, 46; Universal/Amblin (Courtesy Kobal) 78; Popperfoto 25, 32, 36; Gareth Price 29, 59; Rex Features Ltd 9, 18, 28, 55, 60L&T, 61BR; The Royal Mint 34; Science Photo Library 62, 65; C & S Thompson 60BL, 61TL&CL; Zefa Pictures Ltd 22.
Cover Photograph: Pictor International

Place value

All these numbers can be written using a single 1 and some 0s. But the numbers are very different. The 1 is in a different position each time. This makes it worth a different amount.

We say the meaning of the number and its box is its **value**. So, a 1 in the tens box has a value of 10. The position of a number is called its **place value**. When you work with numbers, you must write them down in their correct places. Get the figure 1 in the wrong place and a million pound Lottery win can become a single pound coin!

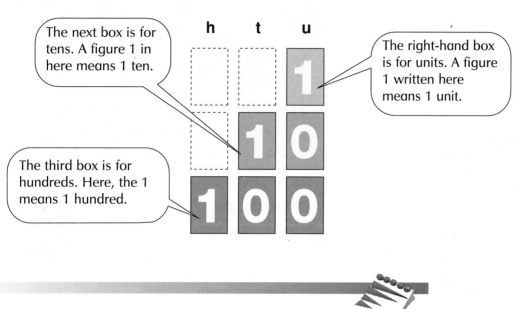

The next box is for tens. A figure 1 in here means 1 ten.

The right-hand box is for units. A figure 1 written here means 1 unit.

The third box is for hundreds. Here, the 1 means 1 hundred.

Draw a line of three empty boxes in your exercise book. Use the diagram above to show you how. Now use the figures 6 and 0 to make as many different numbers as possible.

Give the value of the underlined numbers.
❶ 5<u>8</u>	❹ 1<u>7</u>	❼ <u>5</u>9	❿ <u>1</u>9
❷ <u>4</u>1	❺ <u>8</u>0	❽ <u>7</u>4	⓫ <u>4</u>3
❸ 1<u>3</u>	❻ 3<u>0</u>	❾ 6<u>2</u>	⓬ <u>9</u>8

Give the value of the underlined numbers.
❶ 6<u>7</u>5	❹ 6<u>0</u>9	❼ 6<u>1</u>7	❿ 6<u>2</u>1
❷ <u>8</u>21	❺ 9<u>8</u>2	❽ <u>5</u>82	⓫ 4<u>7</u>9
❸ 75<u>0</u>	❻ <u>1</u>53	❾ 98<u>7</u>	⓬ 56<u>3</u>

1.2 Adding and subtracting

Rush hour in Tokyo! The guards with the white gloves have to push people in to make sure the doors are not blocked. Would you get on or wait for the next train?

- *How many passengers would you tell to get off the train?*
- *What is the most crowded journey you can remember?*

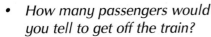

This chart shows how many people get on a train at each stop. No one gets off until they reach the housing area.

Central station	Monument	Business district	Shopping centre	Housing area
75	13	42	51	125 people get off the train

Central station	Monument	Business district	Shopping centre	Housing area

❶ How many people get on the train at the central station?
❷ How many people are on the train after the shopping centre?
❸ How many people are left on the train as it leaves the housing area?

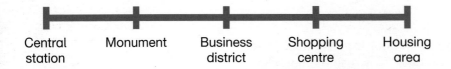

Arrange these sums so that the numbers fit under each other correctly. Then find their total.

❶ $38 + 127 + 16 =$
❷ $58 + 7 + 128 =$
❸ $69 + 407 + 10 =$
❹ $158 + 12 + 132 =$
❺ $671 + 2 + 28 =$

❻ $78 + 721 + 6 =$
❼ $309 + 4 + 28 =$
❽ $521 + 73 + 21 =$
❾ $382 + 9 + 75 =$
❿ $6 + 81 + 483 =$

Adding

143 + 85 + 7

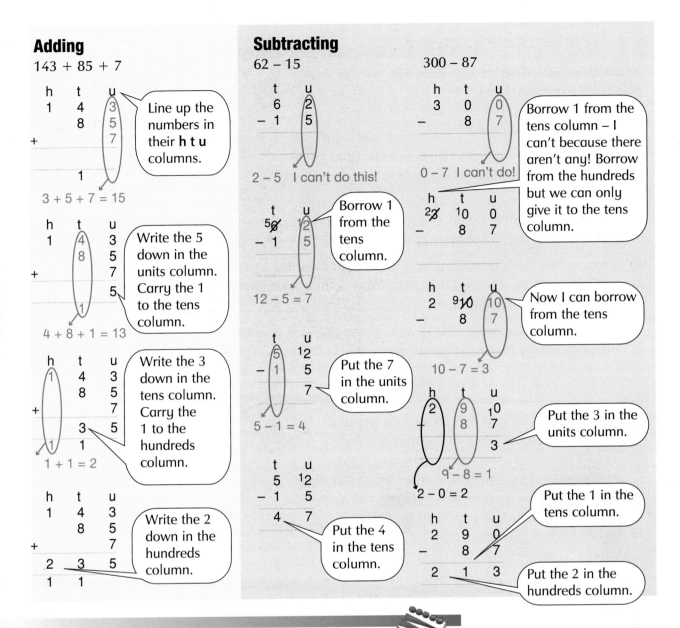

	h	t	u	
	1	4	3	Line up the numbers in their **h t u** columns.
		8	5	
+			7	
			1	

3 + 5 + 7 = 15

	h	t	u	
	1	4	3	Write the 5 down in the units column. Carry the 1 to the tens column.
		8	5	
+			7	
			5	
		1		

4 + 8 + 1 = 13

	h	t	u	
	1	4	3	Write the 3 down in the tens column. Carry the 1 to the hundreds column.
		8	5	
+		3	7	
		3	5	
	1	1		

1 + 1 = 2

	h	t	u	
	1	4	3	Write the 2 down in the hundreds column.
		8	5	
+			7	
	2	3	5	
	1	1		

Subtracting

62 – 15

	t	u	
	6	2	
–	1	5	

2 – 5 I can't do this!

	t	u	
	5 6	12	Borrow 1 from the tens column.
–	1	5	

12 – 5 = 7

	t	u	
	5	12	Put the 7 in the units column.
–	1	5	
		7	

5 – 1 = 4

	t	u	
	5	12	Put the 4 in the tens column.
–	1	5	
	4	7	

300 – 87

	h	t	u	
	3	0	0	Borrow 1 from the tens column – I can't because there aren't any! Borrow from the hundreds but we can only give it to the tens column.
–		8	7	

0 – 7 I can't do!

	h	t	u	
	2 3	10	0	
–		8	7	

	h	t	u	
	2	9 10	10	Now I can borrow from the tens column.
–		8	7	

10 – 7 = 3

	h	t	u	
	2	9	10	Put the 3 in the units column.
–		8	7	
			3	

9 – 8 = 1

	h	t	u	
	2	9	10	Put the 1 in the tens column.
–		8	7	
		1	3	

2 – 0 = 2

	h	t	u	
	2	9	0	Put the 2 in the hundreds column.
–		8	7	
	2	1	3	

What figure goes in the place of the question mark? Show your working. ③

❶ My CD rack will hold 50 CDs. If I already own 27 disks, how many CDs do I need to fill the rack? _____

> 27 + ? = 50

❷ British Airways need to book 300 seats on a flight to make a profit. 179 seats are already booked. How many more need to be booked? _____

> 179 + ? = 300

❸ The RSPCA shelter can house up to 30 stray cats. If they have 17 already, how many more can they take in? _____

> 17 + ? = 30

❹ A couple bought a house ten years ago for £37 500 and sold it last week for £65 000. How much profit did they make? _____

> 37 500 + ? = 65 000

❺ I had £50 to buy some clothes and came home with £16.27. How much did I spend? _____

> £16.27 + ? = £50

Again, you are looking for the figure that goes in place of the question mark.

1. I spent £3 on Lottery tickets and won. I made £7 profit. How much did I win? _____

   ? – £3 = £7

2. I took £270 from my bank and now have £235 left in my account. How much money was in the account to begin with? _____

   ? – £270 = £235

3. My car is now worth £1500. It has dropped in price by £2700 since I bought it. How much did I pay for the car? _____

   ? – £2700 = £1500

4. A football player is now worth only £850 000 after playing badly this season. This is a loss of £25 790 to the club. How much did the club pay for him? _____

   ? – 25 790 = £850 000

5. My shares are now worth £3255 after losing £624 overnight. How much were they worth yesterday? _____

   ? – £624 = £3255

Set up these sums by yourself. Show your working.

1. A lorry's mileage reading at the start of the day was 45 628 miles. At the end of the day it was 45 986 miles. How far did the driver travel that day? _____

2. The original price of a TV was £499.99. I saved £45 in the sale. How much did I pay for the TV? _____

3. My employers gave me a pay rise of £40 per week. My old wage was £175 per week. How much do I earn now? _____

4. A football stadium can hold 42 000 people. If 36 540 tickets have been sold, how many more people do they need to fill the stadium? _____

5. I sold my house for £129 950 and want to buy a new house that costs £175 000. How much do I need to borrow? _____

6. The price of a computer dropped by £100 in a special sale. The original price was £1399. How much was the sale price? _____

7. My car cost me £3500. I also had to pay £100 road tax before I could take it on the road. How much did I have to pay altogether? _____

8. A shop wants to sell 10 000 of a particular toy before closing for Christmas. By December 18th it had sold only 5855. How many more toys will it need to sell to meet its target? _____

9. My life insurance will pay my wife £50 000 if I die. We still owe £37 850 for our mortgage. How much will be left from the insurance payout after the mortgage is paid? _____

1.3 Numbers and words

When you write a cheque, you write down the amount in both numbers and words. This makes it much clearer for the bank – you wouldn't want them to get the amounts wrong!

- *What is the highest value note you have ever seen?*
- *'All our coins say what they are worth in words as well as figures.' Don't look – true or false? Now check.*

Write these words as numbers.

❶ seventy-four
❷ nine
❸ three hundred and fifty-two
❹ one hundred and sixteen
❺ forty-two
❻ twenty-three
❼ sixty-five
❽ six hundred and thirty-seven
❾ eighty-eight
❿ eleven

When you rent somewhere to live you often have to pay money before you move in. If you look after the flat you should get it back when you leave. This money is called a **deposit**. These adverts show the rents and deposits on some flats.

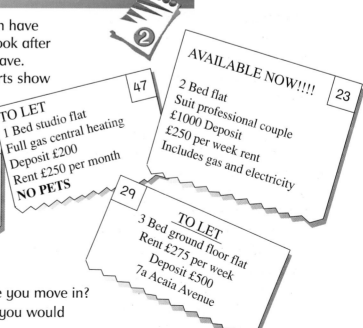

SHARE in house 17
Large house in west of city
5 Beds
Deposit £1500
Rent £850 per week including all bills. **References essential**

TO LET 47
1 Bed studio flat
Full gas central heating
Deposit £200
Rent £250 per month
NO PETS

AVAILABLE NOW!!!! 23
2 Bed flat
Suit professional couple
£1000 Deposit
£250 per week rent
Includes gas and electricity

TO LET 29
3 Bed ground floor flat
Rent £275 per week
Deposit £500
7a Acaia Avenue

❶ Which flat costs the most to rent?
❷ Which flat is the cheapest to rent?
❸ Which flat would cost you £1000 before you move in?
❹ Write down the deposit for each flat as you would have to spell it out on a cheque.

1.4 Getting colder

These pictures show different places on the same day in January. We usually measure temperature in 'degrees Celsius' (°C). On this scale, water freezes at 0°C and boils at 100°C.

- *Where is the coldest place you have been? How cold was it?*
- *Which feels worse to you – too hot or too cold?*

Copy and complete this table of temperature changes.

Starting temperature	Rise in temperature	Final temperature
36°C	12°C	
18°C	4°C	
47°F	17°F	
21°F	43°F	
98°F	21°F	

Copy and complete this table of temperature changes.

Starting temperature	Fall in temperature	Final temperature
31°C	9°C	
78°C	14°C	
45°F	17°F	
226°F	99°F	
108°F	65°F	

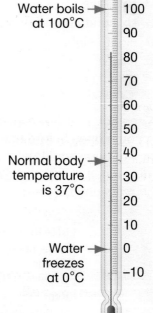

Water boils at 100°C → 100

Normal body temperature is 37°C →

Water freezes at 0°C → 0

110
100
90
80
70
60
50
40
30
20
10
0
−10

Holiday temperatures

When you go on holiday, you want to know roughly what the temperature will be. Will it be warm enough to go swimming? Will it be cold enough for snow? Holiday brochures give the likely temperature for a resort. They cannot be exact – you can't predict the weather! They give approximate figures, perhaps to the nearest 10 degrees. To approximate a number to the nearest 10, use the rules shown by the arrows.

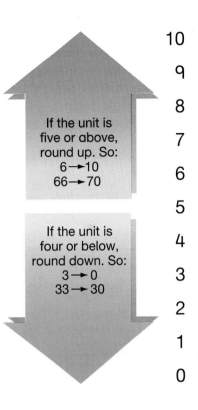

10
9
8

If the unit is five or above, round up. So:
6 → 10
66 → 70

7
6
5

If the unit is four or below, round down. So:
3 → 0
33 → 30

4
3
2
1
0

To the nearest 10, what is the temperature in each of the places shown in the photographs on page 10?

Round each of these numbers off to the nearest 10.

❶ 37
❷ 29
❸ 72
❹ 16
❺ 85
❻ 43
❼ 97
❽ 88
❾ 64
❿ 27
⓫ 99
⓬ 78

Motorbikes and cars

Sometimes rounding numbers to the nearest 100 is accurate enough. A BMW may cost only £24 395 but saying it costs £24 400 is near enough for most people! The rules for rounding numbers to the nearest 100 are the same as for rounding to the nearest 10.

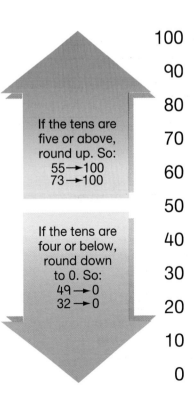

100
90
80

If the tens are five or above, round up. So:
55 → 100
73 → 100

70
60
50

If the tens are four or below, round down to 0. So:
49 → 0
32 → 0

40
30
20
10
0

Round each of these numbers off to the nearest 100.

❶ 287
❷ 128
❸ 689
❹ 223
❺ 550
❻ 485
❼ 732
❽ 611
❾ 333
❿ 459
⓫ 274
⓬ 677

1.5 Number patterns

A lot of the numbers you meet are arranged in patterns. If you can spot the pattern you can fill in missing numbers or predict what will come next. These patterns often depend on adding or subtracting the same number over and over again.

- *What number is hidden behind the lorry?*
- *What colour is the door to number 15?*

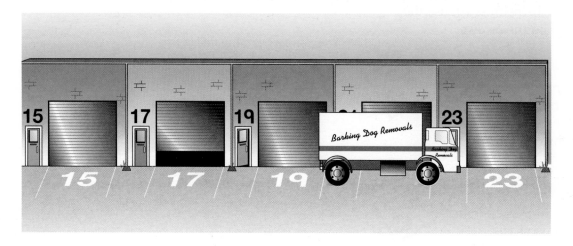

To find the pattern in a sequence of numbers look at the **differences** between numbers. If the differences are the same each time you can predict the next number in the sequence.

This is the number sequence.

Your mystery number.

17   19   21   (?)   25   27
 ↘2↗ ↘2↗ ↘2↗ ↘2↗ ↘2↗

These are the differences between the numbers in your sequence.

These are predictions from the simple pattern.

For more complicated sequences you may need to use more lines of differences.

1   4   10   19   31   45
 ↘3↗ ↘6↗ ↘9↗ ↘12↗ ↘15↗
   ↘3↗ ↘3↗ ↘3↗ ↘3↗

Use this line to predict the line above.

You can use the line of three to predict the next line up.

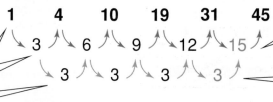

Add three new numbers to continue these number patterns.

❶ 12 22 32 42
❷ 10 17 24 31
❸ 5 7 9 11
❹ 6 14 22 30
❺ 3 14 25 36
❻ 18 21 24 27
❼ 14 20 26 32
❽ 36 39 42 45

Add three new numbers to these number patterns.

1. 90 80 70 60
2. 100 94 88 82
3. 67 62 57 52
4. 98 89 80 71
5. 84 72 60 48
6. 97 90 83 76
7. 87 81 75 69
8. 64 61 58 53

Filling the gaps

The scale on a measuring jug is marked in regular intervals but not all the marks are numbered. Why do you think some of the marks are not labelled?

1. Draw a copy of the scale and fill in the missing numbers.
2. Mark the place where the liquid would come up to if you poured 375 ml into the jug.

Saving up

Each stamp on a TV licence savings card costs £1. People try to predict when their card will be full. Then they can trade it in for a TV licence. If you buy three stamps every week, how many will you have after five weeks?

Week	1	2	3	4	5
Stamps	3	6	9	12	15

1. Use the pattern to predict how many stamps you will have after nine weeks.
2. How much money will these stamps be worth?
3. I buy two stamps every week. There are 52 weeks in a year. How much money will I save in a year?
4. Will this be enough to pay my TV licence? It costs £105.

1.6 Pot black

When you play for big money, you keep track of which balls are left on the table. You add up your score in your head as you go along. You also add up how many points are left on the table. Each colour is worth a different number of points.

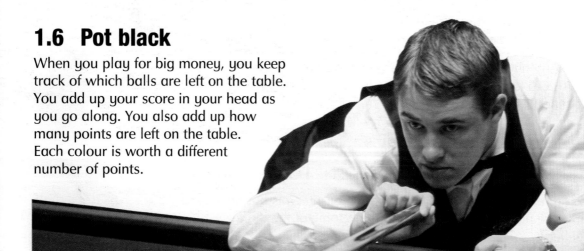

- *Why do you think people like watching snooker on television?*
- *How many hours a day do you think you would have to practise to be as good as Stephen Hendry?*

Work out the scores for each of the breaks below. Do the sums in your head – just write down the answers.

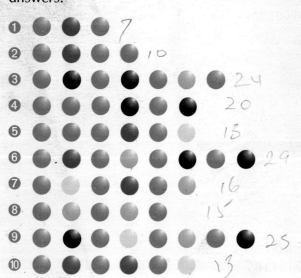

1. 7
2. 10
3. 24
4. 20
5. 13
6. 29
7. 16
8. 15
9. 25
10. 13

1
2
3
4
5
6
7

One hundred and eighty!

Here is another time when you need to add and subtract numbers in your head. Everyone starts at 501 and takes away the points they score. First to zero is the winner! You need to add up the scores for your three darts. Then you subtract the total from your score.

Work out the scores for each of the sets of darts below. Then take the score away from 501. Do the sums in your head – just write down the answers.

2 Using a calculator

2.1 Adding and subtracting

Films often show computers as very large machines. In fact, even a pocket-sized calculator contains a tiny computer. And computers that would fill a room thirty years ago are not as powerful as today's hand-held devices.

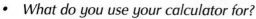

- *What do you use your calculator for?*
- *What else would you like your calculator to be able to do? Why?*

A calculator or not?

Some people use a calculator for every sum. You need to think about whether a sum needs a calculator or if it is easier to do in your head. Sometimes using a calculator takes more time than doing it in your head. Always think before you reach for the calculator – is this the easiest way to do it?

> Calculators just make sums easier – they give you more time to think.

> I only use my calculator for really awkward sums. The simple ones are quicker to do in my head.

> Calculators make you stupid – you never need to work out sums for yourself.

> I use a calculator to check my sums.

> Most of the time I don't need a calculator – a rough answer is all I need.

Different calculators have different buttons. Some are very complicated. They all have the basic functions – usually in the same place.

Most calculators use batteries for power. Some also have solar cells which generate electricity and make the batteries last longer.

PLUS TEC
DUAL POWER
2 POWER

2.1

This display shows the numbers.

These buttons use the calculator's memory for more complicated calculations.

This button switches on the calculator. It also clears any numbers already loaded in to the calculator so that you can start a new calculation. It is often orange in colour.

The buttons used to enter the numbers are usually in the same pattern on every calculator.

These buttons tell the calculator what to do with the numbers you add. Often they act as an equals button as well. So, if you press 2 + 2 the display will show 4 even before you press the = button.

This is the decimal point. You do not need to press this unless there is a number after it.

Press this button to give the answers to your calculation.

Complete the following.

1. $21 + 17 + 93 + 42 + 63 + 82 + 5 + 16 + 26 + 30 =$
2. $37 + 23 + 18 + 56 + 71 + 80 + 19 + 8 + 31 + 29 =$
3. $22 + 3 + 7 + 18 + 98 + 76 + 68 + 54 + 2 + 81 =$
4. $93 + 84 + 75 + 66 + 57 + 48 + 39 + 3 + 17 + 11 =$
5. $94 + 73 + 16 + 21 + 5 + 9 + 62 + 23 + 14 + 12 =$
6. $99 + 23 + 86 + 71 + 42 + 31 + 20 + 4 + 1 + 27 =$
7. $34 + 71 + 16 + 23 + 19 + 8 + 72 + 3 + 9 + 15 =$
8. $64 + 33 + 26 + 41 + 18 + 6 + 75 + 17 + 91 + 6 =$
9. $5 + 17 + 28 + 39 + 85 + 73 + 61 + 8 + 49 + 7 =$
10. $11 + 23 + 13 + 74 + 53 + 88 + 20 + 46 + 81 + 68 =$

Complete the following.

1. $78 - 13 =$
2. $27 - 19 =$
3. $94 - 76 =$
4. $57 - 43 =$
5. $86 - 29 =$
6. $31 - 8 =$
7. $44 - 27 =$
8. $98 - 72 =$
9. $62 - 49 =$
10. $74 - 16 =$

2.2 Multiplying

Every year hundreds of people are rescued by the emergency services. Hundreds of lives are saved across the whole country.

- *Have you ever been in a situation where you needed to be rescued?*
- *Would you want to work in a rescue team? Why? Why not?*

There are eight rescuers in a typical team. Each one has a torch with three high-power batteries. The batteries are replaced every fortnight to make sure they are always in top condition. How many batteries would you need for the whole team?

You could add 3 and 3 eight times. That's once for each person.

$3 + 3 + 3 + 3 + 3 + 3 + 3 + 3 = 24$

An easier way is to multiply 3 by 8. You end up with the same answer.

$3 \times 8 = 24$

Complete the following.

1. $18 \times 7 =$ 6. $57 \times 75 =$ 11. $22 \times 17 =$
2. $34 \times 27 =$ 7. $83 \times 14 =$ 12. $37 \times 41 =$
3. $61 \times 39 =$ 8. $77 \times 34 =$ 13. $39 \times 12 =$
4. $99 \times 99 =$ 9. $63 \times 48 =$ 14. $66 \times 64 =$
5. $46 \times 24 =$ 10. $90 \times 73 =$ 15. $49 \times 91 =$

Multiplying – the easy way!

Some people can multiply numbers up to 10 in their heads. It's called knowing your tables. The multiplication grid shows the answers you get when you multiply the numbers at the edges of the grid together. Someone has worked out all the sums so you end up with a grid of answers. Make sure you know how to use it.

	1	2	3	4	5
1	1	2	3	4	5
2	2	4	6	8	10
3	3	6	9	12	

To multiply 3 by 2 look along the top to find the 3 and then drag down the column to the row for 2. The answer is 6.

Draw a complete multiplication grid for the numbers up to 10.

Use your multiplication grid to solve these problems.

1. $7 \times 8 =$ 6. $3 \times 8 =$
2. $5 \times 9 =$ 7. $8 \times 9 =$
3. $10 \times 6 =$ 8. $6 \times 7 =$
4. $4 \times 9 =$ 9. $8 \times 4 =$
5. $7 \times 7 =$ 10. $9 \times 9 =$

19

2.3 Decimals

Which side will win? If you add up the players' weights on each side you might get a clue.

- *Have you ever played in a rugby team? Did you win?*
- *Where else might you balance weights to make a contest fair?*

The weights are given in kilograms to one decimal point. Decimals give us place values below one unit. So, 0.1 means one tenth of a whole unit. They are positioned in the opposite way to the place values that read units, tens and hundreds.

To show the difference between numbers on each side of the decimal point we say them in different ways. So, 111 is 'one hundred and eleven' but 1.11 is 'one point one one' not 'one point eleven'.
The decimal point is just as important as the figures. Get it in the wrong place and a heavy 100 kg weight could become a lightweight 1.00 kg – about the weight of a bag of sugar!

Getting bigger • Getting smaller

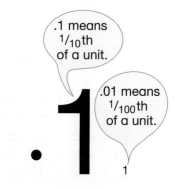

1. means 1 unit – but we don't normally put the decimal point in if there is no number after it.

.1 means 1/10th of a unit.

.01 means 1/100th of a unit.

The reading is 70.5 kg.

Write down the value shown on each of these scales. You will need to use a decimal point in each one.

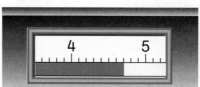
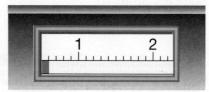

Calculating with decimals

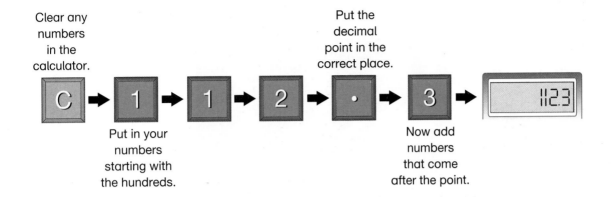

Clear any numbers in the calculator.

Put in your numbers starting with the hundreds.

Put the decimal point in the correct place.

Now add numbers that come after the point.

Complete the following.

1. $9.4 + 7.1 + 83.27 + 2.04 + 0.3 =$
2. $0.01 + 72.3 + 11.42 + 90.81 + 6.9 =$
3. $4.78 + 8.45 + 3.8 + 67.1 + 13.03 =$
4. $14.5 + 28.53 + 28.04 + 81.7 + 16.05 =$
5. $42.8 + 89.4 + 31.6 + 0.74 + 65.8 =$
6. $10.5 + 95.3 + 7.93 + 3.14 + 46.03 =$
7. $1.81 + 18.1 + 0.181 + 0.0181 + 18.01 =$
8. $67.2 + 2.76 + 76.2 + 7.26 + 0.762 =$
9. $10.89 + 16.2 + 98.01 + 17.3 + 8.14 =$
10. $30.7 + 9.02 + 3.16 + 0.04 + 12.78 =$

Complete the following.

1. $7.8 - 0.13 =$
2. $2.7 - 1.9 =$
3. $19.4 - 0.76 =$
4. $5.7 - 1.43 =$
5. $8.67 - 2.91 =$
6. $31.7 - 8.63 =$
7. $8.44 - 2.71 =$
8. $29.8 - 7.23 =$
9. $36.2 - 14.9 =$
10. $74.7 - 16.9 =$

Complete the following.

1. $1.8 \times 3.7 =$
2. $23.4 \times 2.7 =$
3. $61.7 \times 3.9 =$
4. $9.98 \times 3.93 =$
5. $94.6 \times 24.2 =$
6. $5.7 \times 0.75 =$
7. $18.3 \times 2.14 =$
8. $7.71 \times 34.2 =$
9. $6.37 \times 2.48 =$
10. $90.4 \times 7.31 =$

2.4 Dividing and fractions

Every expedition needs to take supplies. These need to be divided so that everyone carries a fair share. Dividing is the opposite of multiplying. This expedition took eight tents and divided them between the four rafts. You divide to find the answer to questions like 'How many tents in each raft?'.

- *Where would you like to explore? Why?*
- *Exploring now is a waste of money. We already know where everything is! Do you agree? Why?*

Complete the following.

❶ $56 \div 2 =$ ❺ $27 \div 2 =$ ❾ $49 \div 2 =$
❷ $74 \div 2 =$ ❻ $83 \div 2 =$ ❿ $76 \div 2 =$
❸ $68 \div 2 =$ ❼ $94 \div 2 =$ ⓫ $34 \div 2 =$
❹ $38 \div 2 =$ ❽ $26 \div 2 =$ ⓬ $85 \div 2 =$

Complete the following.

❶ $56 \div 4 =$ ❺ $27 \div 4 =$ ❾ $49 \div 4 =$
❷ $74 \div 4 =$ ❻ $83 \div 4 =$ ❿ $76 \div 4 =$
❸ $68 \div 4 =$ ❼ $94 \div 4 =$ ⓫ $87 \div 4 =$
❹ $38 \div 4 =$ ❽ $26 \div 4 =$ ⓬ $32 \div 4 =$

Complete the following.

❶ $55 \div 5 =$ ❺ $45 \div 5 =$ ❾ $39 \div 5 =$
❷ $60 \div 5 =$ ❻ $85 \div 5 =$ ❿ $76 \div 5 =$
❸ $69 \div 5 =$ ❼ $91 \div 5 =$ ⓫ $35 \div 5 =$
❹ $47 \div 5 =$ ❽ $26 \div 5 =$ ⓬ $97 \div 5 =$

Complete the following.

❶	56 ÷ 8 =	❹	38 ÷ 8 =	❼	95 ÷ 8 =	❿	70 ÷ 8 =
❷	72 ÷ 8 =	❺	27 ÷ 8 =	❽	26 ÷ 8 =	⓫	37 ÷ 8 =
❸	48 ÷ 8 =	❻	82 ÷ 8 =	❾	47 ÷ 8 =	⓬	46 ÷ 8 =

④

Complete the following.

❶	70 ÷ 10 =	❹	55 ÷ 10 =	❼	99 ÷ 10 =	❿	56 ÷ 10 =
❷	90 ÷ 10 =	❺	27 ÷ 10 =	❽	26 ÷ 10 =	⓫	67 ÷ 10 =
❸	78 ÷ 10 =	❻	81 ÷ 10 =	❾	89 ÷ 10 =	⓬	54 ÷ 10 =

⑤

Complete the following.

❶	500 ÷ 100 =	❺	320 ÷ 100 =	❾	49 ÷ 100 =
❷	700 ÷ 100 =	❻	283 ÷ 100 =	❿	56 ÷ 100 =
❸	650 ÷ 100=	❼	954 ÷ 100 =	⓫	777 ÷ 100 =
❹	380 ÷ 100 =	❽	646 ÷ 100 =	⓬	963 ÷ 100 =

⑥

Complete the following.

❶	80 ÷ 5 =	❹	69 ÷ 23 =	❼	96 ÷ 67 =	❿	56 ÷ 7 =
❷	72 ÷ 8 =	❺	74 ÷ 37 =	❽	90 ÷ 18 =	⓫	81 ÷ 9 =
❸	85 ÷ 17 =	❻	81 ÷ 3 =	❾	99 ÷ 3 =	⓬	2047 ÷ 23 =

⑦

Fractions

When you divide something into equal pieces each piece is a
fraction of the whole.

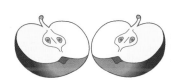

An apple sliced down
the middle should give
two equal halves.

The cake cut into
four equal pieces
gives four quarters.

This bar of chocolate
can be divided into ten
equal pieces. These
are called tenths.

In this Lottery
syndicate of three
people the winnings
are split into thirds.

What fraction of the whole is the black section in the drawings below?

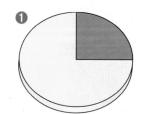 ❶

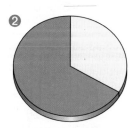 ❷

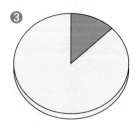 ❸

 ❹

❺ 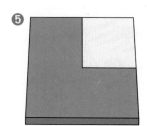 ❻ ❼ 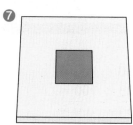 ❽

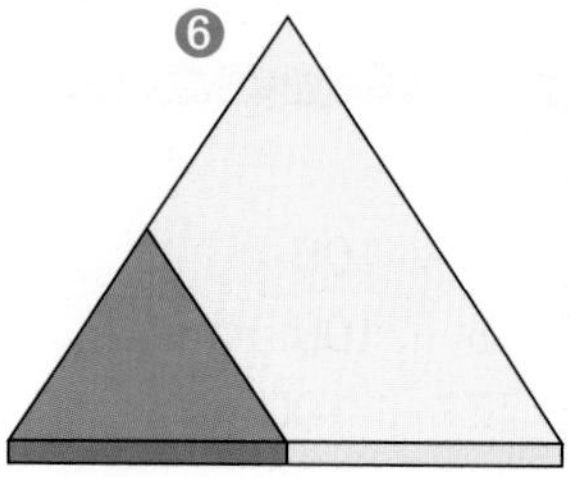

To find a half (½) of any amount on a calculator you can divide by two. To find a quarter (¼) you divide by four. How could you find a sixth (⅙)?
Use your calculator to find:

❶ ½ of 478
❷ ¼ of 616
❸ ⅙ of £32.48
❹ ¼ of 68 cm
❺ ⅙ of 176 kg

❻ ½ of 562 cl
❼ ¼ of 4008
❽ ⅙ of 728 mm
❾ ½ of 998 g
❿ ¼ of £26 000

To find three quarters (¾) of any amount on a calculator you divide by four and then multiply by three.
16 ÷ 4 = 4
4 × 3 = 12
so, ¾ of 16 = 12
Use your calculator to find the following.

❶ ¾ of 96
❷ ⅔ of £66.60
❸ ⅕ of £105.55
❹ ⅔ of 963 g
❺ ⅘ of £1200

❻ ⅗ of 775 mm
❼ ⅓ of 3009 g
❽ ¹⁄₁₀ of 9010 mm
❾ ⁷⁄₁₀ of 50 kg
❿ ⁹⁄₁₀ of £3970

2.5 Rich spice?

If you work in a group you may be paid as a group. How can you make sure everyone gets their fair share?

- *Do you think everyone in the photo should get equal shares? Why? Why not?*
- *What is the largest amount of money you have ever had to share out?*
- *Was everyone happy with your way of sharing it?*

① Share the following amounts of money between two people.

❶ £7.00	❹ £17.80	❼ £3.60	❿ £67.38
❷ £5.00	❺ £23.80	❽ £72.40	⓫ £46.46
❸ £98.00	❻ £28.60	❾ £18.36	⓬ £181.30

② Share the following amounts of money between four people.

❶ £8.00	❹ £48.80	❼ £3.20	❿ £66.24
❷ £10.00	❺ £28.60	❽ £72.40	⓫ £37.84
❸ £88.00	❻ £58.60	❾ £28.36	⓬ £91.36

③ Share the following amounts of money between five people.

❶ £10.00	❹ £17.50	❼ £13.80	❿ £69.35
❷ £5.00	❺ £22.50	❽ £72.05	⓫ £36.80
❸ £95.00	❻ £48.60	❾ £18.45	⓬ £94.25

Share the following amounts of money between 10 people.

① £9.00   ④ £17.00   ⑦ £7.60   ⑩ £57.30
② £15.00   ⑤ £33.00   ⑧ £72.40   ⑪ £47.90
③ £58.00   ⑥ £27.60   ⑨ £8.30   ⑫ £69.20

Making more money

Footballers often get paid more if they score a goal. In the Premier League some players get a bonus of £1000 for every goal they score! Suppose they score two goals in a match. What is the total bonus for a player who scores five goals in the cup competition?

Complete the following.

① £1.48 × 3 =   ⑥ £6.77 × 5 =
② £0.32 × 12 =   ⑦ £11.16 × 50 =
③ £49.12 × 27 =   ⑧ £16.32 × 15 =
④ £7.96 × 48 =   ⑨ £5.94 × 17 =
⑤ £33.20 × 14 =   ⑩ £6.07 × 29 =

Show your working out clearly for each of these questions.

1. A large tub of popcorn at the cinema costs £2.85. If three friends share the popcorn, how much will they pay each?_____

   $2.85 \div 3 = ?$

2. Eight people want a portion of fish and chips each. If one portion costs £2.10 how much money will the total bill come to? _____

   $8 \times 2.10 = ?$

3. Five friends each won £65.00. How much did they win altogether? _____

   $5 \times 65 = ?$

4. Four people shared the Lottery jackpot of £10 000 000. How much did they each receive? _____

   $10\ 000\ 000 \div 4 = ?$

5. A firm arranges an annual trip to a theme park for its employees and their families – a total of 216 people. If a coach can seat 54 people, how many coaches will need to be booked for the trip?_____

   $216 \div 54 = ?$

6. If the cost of entry into the theme park is £7.50 per person, how much will it cost the firm for everybody to get in? _____

   $216 \times 7.5 = ?$

7. A horse can eat a bale of hay in three days. How long will 24 bales last? _____

   $24 \times 3 = ?$

8. A typist is paid £2.50 for typing one page of a book. How much would the typist be paid for typing 16 pages?_____

   $16 \times 2.5 = ?$

9. The journey from Manchester to London is 250 miles. If I travel there and back five times how far have I travelled? _____

   $250 \times 5 = ?$

10. I get paid £2.25 for washing a car. How much will I earn if I wash 17 cars? _____

    $2.25 \times 17 = ?$

Supermarkets often have special prices if you buy more than one of something. Are these offers always the bargains they seem?

1. How much does one bottle cost?
2. How much does the bargain four-pack cost?
3. How much does this work out for each bottle in the pack?
4. How much have you saved per bottle?

4-pack £1.99   3 litres £0.69

27

2.6 Temperatures

The coldest welcome anywhere! This hotel is made of ice – if it warms up, the bedroom becomes a pool! People pay a fortune to stay at this exclusive place – and none of the rooms have showers or baths.

- *Why do you think people will pay to stay at such a strange hotel?*
- *What other sorts of strange hotels can you think of?*

Copy out and complete the following temperature table.

①

	Starting temperature / °C	Rise in temperature / °C	Final temperature / °C
a	−5	22	
b	−9	8	
c	−21	17	
d	−68	70	
e	−4	4	
f	−17	20	
g	−29	40	
h	−11	8	
i	−52	60	
j	13	9	

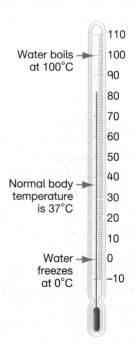

Water boils → 110
at 100°C 100
90
80
70
60
50
Normal body → 40
temperature 30
is 37°C 20
10
Water → 0
freezes
at 0°C −10

Copy out and complete the following temperature table.

Starting temperature / °C	Fall in temperature / °C	Final temperature / °C
10	12	
29	38	
31	32	
8	14	
0	10	
1	12	
17	22	
11	15	
20	30	
6	9	

If it is windy the temperature outside feels colder than if the air is still. This effect is called wind chill. A wind chill factor of minus five means that it will feel as if it is 5°C colder than it actually is.

This college trip started on a bright sunny day. In the valley the temperature was a warm 12°C.
At the mountain top the wind chill of minus eight made it a lot cooler!

❶ What temperature does it feel like on the mountain top?

❷ As the sun goes down the wind stays the same but the valley temperature drops to 5°C. How would it feel on the mountain top at night?

2.7 Constant function addition

If you want people to believe your story, make sure you get the evidence. If I had a pound for every time someone tells me they caught a big fish I'd be a very rich man!

- *What is the most unlikely story you have ever heard?*
- *Do you think men or women are more likely to tell 'tall tales'? Why?*

Calculators have a shortcut to let you add the same number over and over again. This is called the constant function. The flow chart shows how to use it.
Every time you press the = sign you should get a new number.
If you've done it correctly you should see:

5   10   15   20   25

❶ Imagine you could get five pounds for every time the word 'the' is used on these two pages. How much do you think you would get?
❷ Now use the constant function on your calculator to see how close you were.

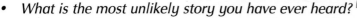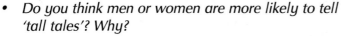

Using the constant function on your calculator, complete the next three numbers in these patterns.

❶	6	12	18	24		❻	12	24	36	48
❷	4	8	12	16		❼	8	16	24	32
❸	3	6	9	12		❽	17	34	51	68
❹	7	14	21	28		❾	9	18	27	36
❺	15	30	45	60		❿	13	26	39	52

Press the five button for your first 'the'.

Press the addition button twice.

Press the five button again for your next 'the'.

Press the equals sign to add the numbers.

Now press the equals button again every time you see the word 'the'.

Keep going until you've finished.

Using number patterns

We can use number patterns to help us solve problems. A calculator is useful to do some of the sums for us while we search for the patterns.

A gardener wants to plant a border of mixed plants. He has designed a row so that it has a white plant between every blue plant. He always starts and finishes with a white plant. How many of each colour does he need?

❶ How many white plants does he need if he has three blue plants?

❷ How many if he has seven blues?

❸ Copy and complete this table. You may find the constant button on your calculator useful to work out the numbers.

Blue flowers	White flowers
1	2
2	3
3	
4	
5	
6	
7	

❹ What patterns can you see in the numbers here?

❺ How many white flowers are needed if there are 10 blue ones?

❻ How many white flowers are needed if there are 20 blue ones?

The gardener knows there is a 100 metre border to plant. He can fit three plants in each metre.

❼ How many plants does he need in total?

❽ How many white plants?

❾ How many blue plants?

The gardener also wants to build a fence with 45 wooden panels. The fence needs a post at both ends.

❶ Use the same pattern for working out the number of fence posts he needs.

❷ The posts cost £5.95 each. How much will the posts cost in total?

❸ The panels cost £7.95 each. How much will the panels cost in total?

❹ The gardener charges £200 for doing the job on top of the costs of the materials. What is the total cost for the fence?

3 Money management

3.1 Small change

This busker will bring home a collection of coins every day. Imagine how long he will need to convert his takings into a single sum of money.

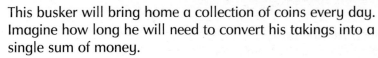

- *Some people think buskers are a nuisance. Do you agree? Why?*
- *What is the most unusual busker you have ever seen?*

Find the total value of these coins.

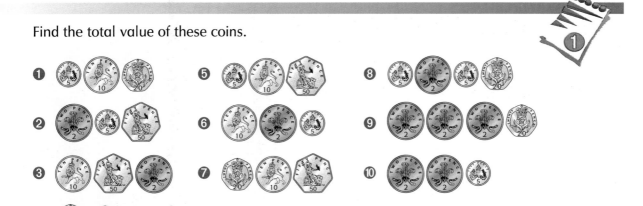

Find the total value of these coins.

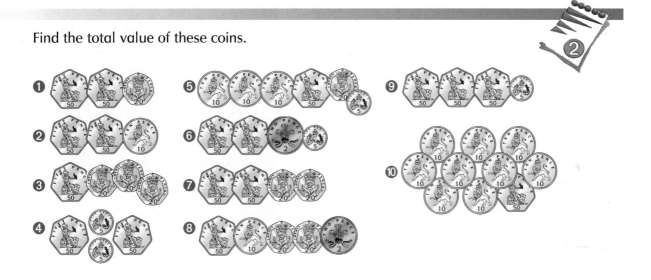

Looking after the pounds

It can be difficult to add up mixtures of different coins. The first step is usually to group them into useful amounts. Pennies can be grouped into piles worth ten pence. Ten pence coins are often grouped into piles worth one pound.

Find ten different ways to make £1 using any of the coins below.

3.2 Cash machines

The Mint makes thousands of coins every day.
These disks are going to be two pence pieces.

- *How many coins do you think are in each drum?*
- *How much would one hundred pounds' worth of two pence pieces weigh?*

A bank gets a delivery of two pence pieces in bags. Each bag contains a pound. How many coins are there in each bag?

Convert the pound into pennies. £1.00 = 100p

↓

Divide the number of pence by two. 100/2 = 50

↓

There are 50 coins in each one pound bag.

State the number of two pences that are needed to make the following amounts of money.

❶ £0.20	❹ £0.84	❼ £3.44	❿ £4.86
❷ £0.36	❺ £2.40	❽ £1.76	⓫ £5.76
❸ £1.00	❻ £1.28	❾ £3.10	⓬ £4.32

State the number of five pences that are needed to make the following amounts of money.

❶ £0.85	❹ £3.85	❼ £2.05	❿ £6.00
❷ £3.75	❺ £1.45	❽ £0.95	⓫ £6.35
❸ £2.50	❻ £5.00	❾ £3.10	⓬ £8.90

State the number of ten pences that are needed to make the following amounts of money.

❶ £0.85 ❹ £3.80 ❼ £2.80 ❿ £6.60
❷ £3.75 ❺ £9.40 ❽ £8.70 ⓫ £7.70
❸ £1.50 ❻ £5.50 ❾ £7.10 ⓬ £9.30

Cashing up

If you win a lot of penny coins in the arcade you will probably want to change them into pounds. It makes it easier to carry your winnings away! One hundred pennies equals one pound.
You write this as 100p=£1. 125 pennies = one pound and twenty-five pennies left over. You write this as 125p=£1.25.

Usually people end up putting money into one-armed bandits! If each go costs a penny how many goes can you have for 45p?

125p	➡	£1 and 25p	➡	£1.25
Start with the number of pennies.		Move the last two figures slightly – these are the pennies. Everything else is in pounds.		Put a decimal point to show the gap between pounds and pennies. Cross out the p sign now.
74623p	➡	£746 and 23p	➡	£746.23
£37.43	➡	37.43	➡	3743p
Start with the pounds and pennies.		Cross out the £ sign.		Take out the decimal point and add a p sign. Now everything is in pennies.
£0.93	➡	0.93	➡	93p
				If you have a zero before the decimal point – cross it out now.

Convert these amounts of money from pence to pounds and pence.

❶ 230 pence ❻ 550 pence
❷ 120 pence ❼ 870 pence
❸ 158 pence ❽ 70 pence
❹ 472 pence ❾ 209 pence
❺ 300 pence ❿ 721 pence

Convert these amounts of money from pounds and pence to pence.

❶ £2.98 ❹ £0.86 ❼ £3.35 ❿ £5.99
❷ £1.56 ❺ £0.50 ❽ £1.08 ⓫ £7.54
❸ £1.20 ❻ £8.12 ❾ £5.01 ⓬ £4.70

3.3 Money and calculators

You can buy almost anything over the INTERNET nowadays! The prices are in pounds and pence but there is no pound sign printed on the list. The pounds are shown before the decimal point. The pence come after the decimal point. Calculators and shop tills often show money in the same way.

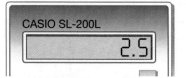

2.5 on your calculator means two pounds and fifty pence. You write this as £2.50 – you must show the zero when you write down the figure.

5.06 means five pounds and six pence. You write this as £5.06 – the zero must be in the same place as it is on the calculator.

CASIO SL-200L

0.65

0.65 means no pounds and sixty-five pence. You can write this as £0.65 or 65p.

Netscape: BIKE IT Home

Bike	
Rear wheel	
Rear axle	45.99
Tyre (black)	32.99
Tyre (whitewall)	17.99
Mirror (small)	21.99
Mirror (large)	8.45
Stem for large mirror	11.25
Badges (small)	3.95
Badges (medium)	3.75
Badges (large)	4.75
	7.95

Never use a £ sign and a p sign in the same figure. You can use just the p sign if there are no pounds – but then do not add any £ signs or any decimal points.

A calculator display showed these answers for questions about money. What do they mean?

❶ 3.86	❹ 7.54	❼ 7.08	❿ 4.09
❷ 6.7	❺ 3.5	❽ 2.9	⓫ 8.58
❸ 1.2	❻ 4.7	❾ 1.8	⓬ 6.3

A calculator display showed these answers for questions about money. What do they mean?

❶ 0.35	❹ 0.65	❼ 0.08	❿ 0.09
❷ 0.48	❺ 0.6	❽ 0.05	⓫ 0.74
❸ 0.84	❻ 0.3	❾ 0.4	⓬ 0.5

3.4 Getting the right change

Car boot sales started in the USA. This couple sell homemade jam and honey for rock-bottom prices.

- *Have you ever bought anything at a car boot sale? What was it?*
- *Sometimes the prices are not marked on the items. Why do you think the sellers leave the price off?*

How much change would you receive from £1 if you buy items costing the following?

❶ 45p 55	❹ 84p	❼ 18p	❿ 4p
❷ 17p 83	❺ 28p	❽ 61p	⓫ 66p
❸ 9p 91	❻ 72p	❾ 44p	⓬ 91p

How much change would you receive from £5 if you buy items costing the following?

❶ £1.50 3.50	❹ £4.65	❼ £2.06	❿ £2.63
❷ £3.95 1.05	❺ £3.19	❽ £4.12	⓫ £3.74
❸ £2.99 2.01	❻ £1.72	❾ £1.39	⓬ £4.89

How much change would you receive from £10 if you buy items costing the following?

❶ £4.75 5.25	❹ £4.99	❼ £7.55	❿ £8.85
❷ £5.95 4.05	❺ £8.82	❽ £6.95	⓫ £1.47
❸ £2.45 7.55	❻ £9.58	❾ £4.05	⓬ £3.65

3.5 Shopping lists

Vegetables cost less on the market – you can get some real bargains! If you do your shopping late on Saturday the prices often go even lower.

- *Where do you buy your fruit and veg?*
- *If market stalls are cheaper why do many people buy their vegetables from supermarkets?*

Add up the shopping bills below. ①

❶
Exercise book	40p
Ruler	50p
Protractor	45p

❷
Pen	25p
Pencil	15p
Rubber	20p

❸
Mars bar	30p
Smarties	29p
Liquorice	4p

❹
Carrots	18p
Apples	85p
Bananas	96p

❺
Milk	35p
Loaf	66p
Teabags	98p

❻
Newspaper	45p
Matches	15p
Pen	30p

Use the photograph to find the total cost of each of the following. ②

❶ One pound of salted cod
❷ A pint of select oysters
❸ Two pounds of smoked herring
❹ Half a pound of select oysters and a claw finger
❺ Three pounds of select oysters and a good oyster knife

Add up the shopping bills below.

①
Shampoo	£2.39
Toothpaste	£1.29
Toothbrush	£1.49

②
CD	£12.99
Magazine	£2.50
Newspaper	£1.30

③
Cheese	£2.57
Pickle	£1.03
Ham	£1.19

④
Dog food	£17.85
Cat food	£2.57
Bird seed	£1.15

⑤
Jumper	£15.99
T-shirt	£9.99
Jeans	£27.99

⑥
Socks	£1.99
Pants	£5.50
Vest	£3.75

⑦
Shoes	£22.99
Bag	£4.99
Scarf	£2.95

Find the total cost of buying the following items from the supermarket.

① A packet of ham, a jar of coffee and a medium white loaf

② Oven chips, a dozen eggs, packet of bacon rashers

③ Tea bags, jar of coffee, 2 litres fresh milk

④ Vegetable stock cubes, chicken breasts, and frozen sweetcorn

⑤ Golden blend, medium white loaf, medium cheddar

⑥ 4 cheese & tomato pizzas, thin pizza and oven chips

⑦ Ice cream, 2 yogurts, white potatoes

⑧ Guardian, spaghetti sauce, drinking chocolate

⑨ Paté slice, Pringles, and medium white loaf

⑩ 2 litre Tango, Wagon Wheels and Harvest chocolate chip bars

PLUSCO

MAGIC ALE	
YOGURT	1.59
YOGURT	0.29
YOGURT	0.29
FRESH MILK (2 pints)	0.29
PRE-PACKED HAM	0.89
THIN PIZZA	1.49
COFFEE	0.99
ICE CREAM	2.75
DRINKING CHOC	2.89
4 CH + TOM PIZZA	1.18
FRZN SWEETCORN	2.19
4 PK LAGER BEER	0.85
COFFEE	5.99
BACON RASHER	2.75
CHICKEN BREASTS	2.49
BKD BEANS (4 pk)	3.75
BKD BEANS (4 pk)	1.32
MED. WHT. LOAF	1.32
MED. WHT. LOAF	0.42
FRESH MILK	0.42
MEDIUM CHEDDAR	0.89
GUARDIAN	2.22
GOLDEN BLEND	0.45
ANGLER LAGER	1.05
OVEN CHIPS	1.99
SPAG SAUCE	1.19
TEA BAGS	1.25
VEG STOCKCUBES	1.65
WHITE POTATO	0.79
DOZ EGGS	1.69
POT NOODLE (6 pk)	1.49
PATE SLICE	2.75
CHOCOLATE CHIP BARS	0.95
TANGO (2 1)	0.85
WAGON WHEELS	1.15
PRINGLES	0.67
	1.25

3.6 What a bargain!

Markets sometimes offer special knock-down prices – a half or even a quarter of what you would pay in the high street shops. But are these prices really bargains?

All tourists should visit the markets. There are some real bargains there – but be prepared to haggle over prices...

- *Are you a keen bargain-hunter in markets and secondhand shops?*
- *What is the best bargain you have ever found?*
- *Where is the best place to find bargains?*

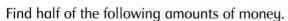

Find half of the following amounts of money.

❶ 56p	❹ 26p	❼ 94p	❿ 98p
❷ 84p	❺ 72p	❽ 36p	⓫ 76p
❸ 38p	❻ 18p	❾ 64p	⓬ 44p

Find half of the following amounts of money.

❶ £3.00	❹ £1.22	❼ £3.28	❿ £168
❷ £2.60	❺ £6.70	❽ £7.66	⓫ £7.98
❸ £1.48	❻ £6.70	❾ £125	⓬ £1.98

Flatmates

SPARKY COMMUNICATIONS

TELEPHONE INVOICE/STATEMENT

Your Account Number
1010   1067069   01/2
Date and Tax Point
31/09/97

Enquiries should be made to our Customer Services Department on: (0123) 123456

The Occupier
Flat 4
17 Main Street
Norwich
NR6 7AQ

FROM	TO	DESCRIPTION	CHARGES/CREDITS
1/06	30/06	TELEPHONE CALL CHARGES	111.16
1/06		TELEPHONE LINE RENTAL	11.98
		TOTAL VAT INCLUDED IN THIS MONTH'S CHARGES 18.34	

ACCOUNT NUMBER	SERVICE PERIOD FROM	TO	CLOSING DATE	DUE DATE	AMOUNT DUE
As above	1/08	31/08	31/08/97	15/09/97	123.14

ADDRESS AT WHICH SERVICE IS PROVIDED
As above

UE United Electricity

Supply to:
The Occupier
Flat 4
17 Main Street
Norwich
NR6 7AQ

METER READINGS

Present	Previous	Units supplied	Domestic	Amount
60197	59741	456	@ 7.22p	£32.92
Fixed charges				£3.22
AMOUNT NOW DUE				£36.14

Four people share this flat. These two bills have just arrived.

③

❶ What is the total that must be paid for the electricity bill?
❷ How much must each person pay?
❸ What is the total amount due for the telephone bill?
❹ How much must each person pay?

④

Find a quarter of the following amounts of money.

❶ 40p ❹ 24p ❼ 60p ❿ 56p
❷ 84p ❺ 76p ❽ 8p ⓫ 88p
❸ 32p ❻ 16p ❾ 92p ⓬ 48p

⑤

Find a quarter of the following amounts of money.

❶ £4.00 ❹ £4.20 ❼ £2.28 ❿ £68.52
❷ £8.40 ❺ £6.60 ❽ £7.36 ⓫ £87.56
❸ £1.40 ❻ £5.44 ❾ £2.27 ⓬ £9.48

4 Clocks and time

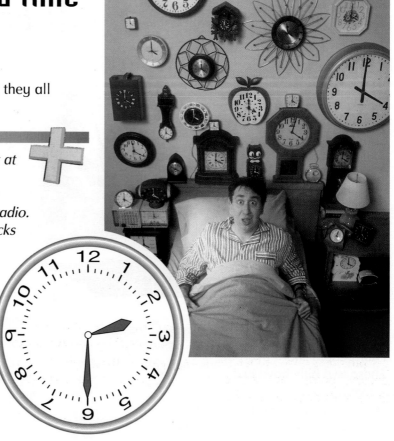

4.1 Clocks

These clocks look very different but they all do the same job.

- *How many clocks have you got at home?*
  Remember to include electronic clocks in the video recorder or radio.
- *What did people use before clocks were invented?*

You can write the time in words or numbers. This clock shows the time of half past two. You could also write this as two thirty or 2:30.

What times do all these clocks say?

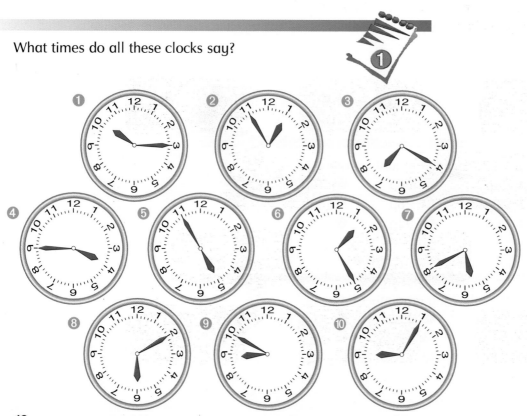

Write the following times in 12 hour time.

1. Quarter past four
2. Half past seven
3. Twenty to nine
4. Quarter to one
5. Ten to ten
6. Twenty-five past three
7. Five past eight
8. Twenty to eleven
9. Twenty-five to one
10. Five to seven

Write these times in words.

1. 6:10
2. 8:45
3. 2:14
4. 10:15
5. 11:35
6. 8:05
7. 3:19
8. 5:33
9. 9:04
10. 6:21

Digital clocks

Digital clocks have no hands so they only show numbers. To show the difference between hours and minutes they use a : symbol. When people copy down times from digital clocks they often use just a decimal point. Try not to do this – you may confuse digital clock times with decimal numbers.

Draw clock faces with hands that show the same times as these digital clocks. Then write the times in words.

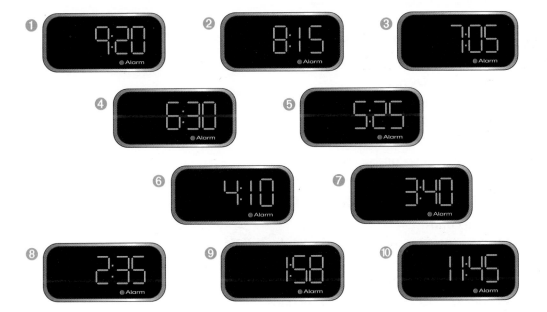

4.2 Hours, minutes and seconds

We've only got 5 minutes before the race starts!

We've only got 300 seconds before the race starts!

0.003 hour pit stop! The Bennetton team can change all the tyres on this car in less than 10 seconds. That's the same as 0.003 hours, but using seconds sounds much more sensible.

- *Are these times the same?*
- *Which would you be more likely to say?*

Convert these times into minutes and seconds.

1. 80 seconds
2. 200 seconds
3. 143 seconds
4. 69 seconds
5. 73 seconds
6. 87 seconds
7. 121 seconds
8. 198 seconds
9. 98 seconds
10. 236 seconds

Convert these times into seconds.

1. 3 minutes 20 seconds
2. 5 minutes 13 seconds
3. 4 minutes 38 seconds
4. 10 minutes 48 seconds
5. 20 minutes 20 seconds
6. 6 minutes 17 seconds
7. 2 minutes 33 seconds
8. 13 minutes 6 seconds
9. 17 minutes 24 seconds
10. 8 minutes 59 seconds

You can buy video tapes that last for different amounts of time. The time they show is always given in minutes. How long will the tapes here last in hours?

Convert these times into hours and minutes.

① 90 minutes 1·30   ⑥ 100 minutes
② 75 minutes 1.15   ⑦ 83 minutes
③ 205 minutes 3·25   ⑧ 62 minutes
④ 63 minutes 1 03   ⑨ 127 minutes
⑤ 138 minutes 2.18   ⑩ 255 minutes

Convert these times into minutes.

① 2 hours 25 minutes 245   ⑥ 6 hours 13 minutes
② 1 hour 14 minutes 74   ⑦ 4 hours 29 minutes
③ 5 hours 36 minutes 336   ⑧ 10 hours 6 minutes
④ 9 hours 7 minutes 671   ⑨ 3 hours 57 minutes
⑤ 11 hours 11 minutes   ⑩ 7 hours 22 minutes

These are the winning times for an athletics competition. Write out the results using more sensible units.

Race	Winning time
100 m	0.217 minutes
400 m	0.02 hours
1500 m	330 seconds
5000 m	2700 seconds
Marathon	260 minutes

How many seconds does this car take to reach 60 mph?

...this little mover will go from a standing start to 60 mph in just 0.07 of a minute...
Super Car   Sept. '97

4.3 Twelve or twenty-four?

Timetables and departure boards often use the 24 hour clock to show times. Numbers smaller than 12 are used for times from midnight to noon. Numbers bigger than 12 are for times in the afternoon and evening.

When we talk about time we often use words like '5 o'clock in the afternoon' or '7 o'clock in the morning'. When we write these we use **am** for times between midnight and noon. We use **pm** for times in the afternoon and evening.

- *Have you ever missed a train because you got the time wrong?*
- *Why do you think train companies use a 24 hour clock?*

LONDON TO PARIS EUROSTAR SCHEDULE		
TRAIN	DEPART	ARRIVE
9006	07.23	11.17
9008	07.53	11.53
9010	08.23	12.23
9014	09.23	13.23
9018	10.23	14.17
9024	11.57	16.05
9028	12.53	16.47
9034	14.23	18.26
9038	15.23	17.23
9042	16.23	20.29
9044	16.53	20.56
9046	17.15	19.20
9048	17.48	19.53
9052	18.53	22.53

11.22 ⇨ ⇨ 11.22 am

If the hour number is lower than 12 do nothing.

Add am to the time – this is a time in the morning.

17.05 ⇨ 5.05 ⇨ 5.05 pm

If the hour number is higher than 12, take away 12.

Add pm to the time – this is a time in the afternoon.

6.32 am ⇨ ⇨ 6.32

If the 12 hour has am – do nothing.

Remove am from the time – this is a time in the morning.

9.17 pm ⇨ 9.17 ⇨ 21.17

If the 12 hour has pm – remove the pm.

Now add 12 to the hours – this is a time in the afternoon.

PARIS TO LONDON EUROSTAR SCHEDULE		
TRAIN	DEPART	ARRIVE
9007	07.16	09.09
9011	08.13	10.13
9015	09.10	11.09
9019	10.19	12.13
9027	12.13	14.13
9027	13.07	15.13
9035	14.16	16.09
9039	15.19	17.13
9043	16.07	18.13
9047	17.10	19.13
9049	17.46	19.43
9051	18.18	20.13
9055	19.19	21.13
9059	20.07	22.13

1. How many trains leave London for Paris before midday?
2. What is the number of the train leaving Paris at 8:13 am?
3. What is the number of the train getting to Paris just before eight o'clock in the evening?
4. I got to Waterloo at 10 o'clock in the morning. What time is the next Eurostar train to Paris?
5. When does train 9034 arrive in Paris?
6. How long does the journey from Paris to London take if I use the 07:16 train from Paris?
7. How many trains leave London after three o'clock in the afternoon?
8. What time does the last train for London leave Paris?

Convert these times to 12 hour.
1. 03:15
2. 17:21
3. 21:17
4. 12:35
5. 00:19
6. 08:45
7. 14:03
8. 01:37
9. 15:16
10. 07:07
11. 18:57
12. 16:10
13. 04:26
14. 20:20
15. 02:45

Convert these times to 24 hour.
1. 8:27 pm
2. 10:15 am
3. 6:25 am
4. 5:45 pm
5. 12:28 am
6. 1:21 am
7. 3:45 pm
8. 5:16 am
9. 10:10 am
10. 9:11 am
11. 7:30 pm
12. 9:26 pm
13. 8:21 am
14. 10:30 pm
15. 11:11 pm

Calculate the time between each of the following.
1. 14:20 and 15:25
2. 11:15 and 21:10
3. 07:17 and 12:03
4. 00:36 and 10:14
5. 19:20 and 23:16
6. 04:32 and 13:20
7. 20:13 and 23:24
8. 10:15 and 17:36
9. 12:18 and 19:07
10. 05:10 and 11:11

4.4 Watching the box

Almost every home in this country has at least one television set. Some have three or four sets! Well, it stops arguments about what to watch!

- How many television sets are there in your home?
- How much do you watch television?

BBC1	BBC2	ITV	Channel 4
7.00 pm NEW SERIES This is Your Life Michael Aspel catches up with another celebrity. *(Txt, S)*	**6.00 pm** The Simpsons Bart discovers love, but will Homer tell him what he needs to know? *(Txt, S)*	**6.00 pm** Granada Tonight	**6.00 pm** The Cosby Show Sitcom from US.
7.30 pm Mastermind, the final	**6.25 pm** Space Precinct Strangest costumes on TV *(S)*	**6.30 pm** The Footie Show When footballers can earn more from appearing in adverts has the game really sold out to commercial pressures?	**6.30 pm** Hollyoaks
8.00 pm EastEnders Grant tries to hide the truth from Peggy. Pauline smiles – but will it last? *(Txt, S)* See feature, p. 9	**7.10 pm** Electric Circuit Pop magazine programme this week featuring Manchester-based band Oasis. *(Txt, S)*		**7.00 pm** News, Weather
8.30 pm Only Fools and Horses Sitcom. The classic episode where Delboy tries to cultivate a yuppie image. *(Txt, Rpt, S)*	**7.30 pm** The Sci Files A look at how science is changing the way we live – and what the future may hold for our children. *(Txt, S)*	**7.00 pm** Wish You Were Here Holiday show. Watch Judith Chalmers testing out a mud bath in Istanbul.	**7.50 pm** Thatcher's Children Documentary series about people born during the Thatcher years.
9.00 pm News, Local News, Weather *(Txt)*	**8.00 pm** Top Gear Motorsport Reports from men in cars. *(Txt, S)*	**7.30 pm** Coronation Street Vera wonders who really does own the Rovers. And what are the police looking for in Mike Baldwin's factory?	**8.00 pm** Mrs. Cohen's Money
9.30 pm NEW SERIES Bloomin' Marvellous Comedy series – the pitfalls of starting a family.	**8.30 pm** The Antiques Show	**8.00 pm** World in Action	**8.30 pm** Brookside
10.00 pm Preston Front	**9.00 pm** Red Dwarf Kryten, Rimmer and Lister stop off on a small planet for a spot of golf. *(Txt, S)*	**8.30 pm** Kavanagh QC The evidence points to a simple, open-and-shut case. So why is Kavanagh worried?	**9.00 pm** The Surgery Series about life in a doctor's surgery in a busy city.
10.40 pm Full Circle Shown yesterday. *(Txt, S)*	**9.45 pm** This Life Egg reaches crisis point and Anna regrets her latest argument with Miles. *(Txt, S)*	**10.00 pm** News, Weather	**10.00 pm** Dark Skies Majestic is closing in – and watch for some clues about who really shot JFK.
11.30 pm NEW SERIES Film 97 with Barry Norman	**10.30 pm** Newsnight *(Txt)*	**10.30 pm** Granada News	**11.00 pm** Armstrong and Miller
	11.30 pm The Kingdom of the Ice Bear	**10.40 pm** Taggart A nasty case of racial abuse that leads to murder for the Scottish dertective.	**11.45 pm** Plasticine People
		11.40 pm FILM: Body parts *See Films on p. 20*	**12.05 am** FILM High Noon

How long do each of these television programmes last?

1. Hollyoaks
2. The Antiques Show
3. Space Precinct
4. Thatcher's Children
5. Full Circle
6. Mastermind, the final
7. Granada News
8. Preston Front
9. The Simpsons
10. Red Dwarf

How long do these groups of programmes last in total?

1. Mastermind, EastEnders and Only Fools and Horses
2. Top Gear and The Antiques Show
3. World in Action and Kavanagh QC
4. Thatcher's Children, Mrs. Cohen's Money and Brookside
5. Red Dwarf, This Life and Newsnight

Your friend has asked you to record EastEnders for her while she is on holiday. She has left you some blank video tapes that are 180 minutes long.

1. How long is an episode of EastEnders?
2. How many episodes will fit on to each tape?
3. There are three episodes of EastEnders each week. How many tapes will you need if your friend is away for a fortnight?

How many editions of the following programmes could you record on a three hour video tape?

1. Top Gear Motorsport
2. The Surgery
3. Kavanagh QC
4. Preston Front
5. Electric Circuit

4.5 The interview

Briggs & Sons

Dear Ms Stevens,

Thank you for your application for the job of office assistant at Briggs and Sons. We would be grateful if you could attend for interview at 11 am on Tuesday May 23rd. Our offices are approximately seven minutes' walk from Headley Mill railway station.

Yours sincerely,

J. Smith

J. Smith
Personnel manager.

LOCALTRAINS TIMETABLE

Fulldale → Leaglass

	SuX	SuX							
Fulldale	0745	0935	1115	1215	1315	1415	1515	1615	1710
Beckton	0747	0937	pu	pu	pu	pu	pu	pu	pu
Middleground	0752	0942	1123	1223	1323	1423	1523	1623	1718
The Green	0755	0945	1128	1228	1328	1428	1528	1628	1723
Castle Road	0800	0950	1135	1235	1335	1435	1535	1635	1730
Headley Mill	0813	1003	1148	1248	1348	1448	1548	1648	1743
Leaglass	0820	1010	1155	1255	1355	1455	1555	1655	1750

Notes: SuX Does not run on Sundays
pu Stops on hand signal to driver to pick up only

Service number	20	20	20	20	19	20	20	20	19 and 20	20	20	20	19	19
Charles Street	0815	0835	0845	0855	-	0905	0915	0925		1805	1835	1935	—	—
Wyngate School	0835	0855	0905	0915	-	0925	0935	0945	At these minutes past the hour until 1800	1825	1855	1955	—	—
Fulldale station	0900	0920	0930	0940	0945	0950	1000	1010		1850	1920	2020	1845	1945
Outdale High St	0935	0955	1005	1015	1015	1025	1035	1045		1925	1955	2055	1915	2015
Imperial Avenue	—	—	—	—	1035	—	—	—		—	—	—	19:35	2035
Walnut Grove	—	—	—	—	1100	—	—	—		—	—	—	2000	2100

- *Have you ever been to an interview? What was it for?*
- *What did you wear?*
- *Did you get there on time?*

Adele Stevens can get to her interview by catching a bus from her home near Wyngate School to Fulldale railway station and then a train to Headley Mill station. She needs to allow plenty of time in case the train is late.

1. Which train will get her to Headley Mill at the best time?
2. What time does this train leave Fulldale?
3. What time must she catch the bus to be sure of catching this train?
4. If it takes her ten minutes to walk to the bus stop, when must she leave home?
5. How long will the whole journey take her?

1. What do the letters SuX mean on the Localtrains timetable?
2. Services 19 and 20 use the same route for two stops. Which stops are these?
3. What time does the 08:15 bus get to Outdale High Street?
4. How many buses would I need to use to get from the stop outside Wyngate School to Imperial Avenue?
5. How many trains travel from Fulldale to Leaglass on Wednesday?
6. How many trains travel from Beckton to Headley Mill on Sunday?
7. If I use the 09:05 bus from Charles Street and catch the earliest possible train from Fulldale station how long will it take to get to Castle Road?

Scotland and North West England → London

Station		1	2	3	4	5	6	7
Inverness	d	—	—	—	—	—	—	—
Perth	d	—	—	—	—	—	0515g	—
Stirling	d	—	—	—	—	—	0549g	0649g
Aberdeen	d	—	—	—	—	—	—	—
Dundee	d	—	—	—	—	—	—	—
Edinburgh	d	—	—	—	0627	—	0650	—
Fort William	d	—	—	—	—	—	—	—
Glasgow Central	d	—	—	0610	—	—	0720	0810
Motherwell	d	—	—	0624	—	—	—	0824
Lockerbie	d	—	—	—	0744	—	—	—
Carlisle	d	0540	—	0635	0735	0820	0842	0939
Penrith	d	0558	—	0652	0752	0839	—	0956
Oxenholme Lake District	d	0624	—	0718	0820	0907	0921	1022
Lancaster	d	0640	0729p	0735	0840	0925	0940	1038
Preston	d	0718	0810d	0818	0918	0955	1018	1059
Wigan North Western	a	0734	0823	0834	0934	1025	—	1115
Warrington Bank Quay	a	0744	0836	0844	0944	—	—	1127
Crewe	a	0806	0904	0914	1010	—	—	1150
Stratford	a	—	—	—	—	—	—	—
Rugby	a	—	—	—	1112	—	—	—
Milton Keynes Central	a	—	—	1027	—	—	—	—
Watford Junction	a	0946s	—	1055s	—	—	1230s	—
London	a	1015	—	1125	1230	—	1305	—

Station		1	2	3	4	5	6	7
Inverness	d	—	—	—	0638e	—	—	—
Perth	d	—	0808g	—	—	0856e	0904g	1008g
Stirling	d	0800g	0840g	—	—	0933e	0940g	1040g
Aberdeen	d	0508g	0627g	—	—	0755e	—	0828g
Dundee	d	—	0745g	—	—	0906e	—	0945g
Einburgh	d	—	—	0850	—	1040	1103	—
Fort William	d	—	—	—	—	—	—	—
Glasgow Central	d	0930	0950	1010	—	—	1103	1140
Motherwell	d	0943	—	1024	—	—	1118	—
Lockerbie	d	—	—	—	—	—	—	—
Carlisle	d	1055	1106	1135	—	1204	1245	1256
Penrith	d	1111	—	1152	—	1220	1304	1313
Oxenholme Lake District	d	1136	—	1218	1224p	1245	1332	1340
Lancaster	d	1200	1155	1235	1245p	1300	1340p	1355
Preston	a	1222	1218	1258	1320d	1320	1406	1418
Wigan North Western	a	1237	1246p	1313	1334	1421p	1436	—
Warrington Bank Quay	a	1252	—	1325	1344	—	—	—
Crewe	a	1314	—	1349	1407	1457	—	—
Stratford	a	1337	—	—	—	1521	—	—
Rugby	a	—	—	—	1505	—	—	—
Milton Keynes Central	a	—	—	—	1530	—	—	—
Watford Junction	a	—	—	—	—	—	—	1627s
London	a	—	1500	—	1625	—	—	1705

Notes specific to this page:
- **B** The Royal Scot
- **X** An InterCity service provided by CrossCountry Trains Ltd.
- **Y** All First Class accommodation is non-smoking. Bicycles cannot be conveyed. Service provided by CrossCountry Trains Ltd.
- **Z** All First Class accommodation is non-smoking.
- **d** departure time
- **e** Change at Edinburgh
- **g** Connection is via Glasgow Queen Street. Customers should make their own way between stations. A weekday daytime bus link is available.
- **p** Change at Preston.
- **s** Stops to set down only.

Newcastle - Middlesbrough - Scarborough - York - Hull - Leeds to Blackpool - Manchester - Manchester Airport - Liverpool

Station	1	2	3	4	5	6	7	8
Sunderland	—	—	1600g	—	—	1630g	1700g	—
Newcastle	—	—	1629f	—	—	1700f	1711	1730f
Chester-le-Street	—	—	1615h	—	—	—	1720	—
Durham	—	—	1642f	—	—	1712f	1728	—
Middlesbrough	—	1612	—	—	—	1713	—	—
Thornaby	—	1617	—	—	—	1718	—	—
Yarm	—	1625	—	—	—	1726	—	—
Darlington	—	—	1700f	—	—	1731f	1747	1757f
Northallerton	—	1644	—	—	—	1745	1800	—
Thirsk	—	1653	—	—	—	1753	1809	—
Scarborough	—	—	1648	—	—	—	—	1759
Seamer	—	—	1653	—	—	—	—	1804
Malton	—	—	1709	—	—	—	—	1820
York a	—	1712	1734	—	—	1813	1832	1844
York d	—	1715	1737	1745	—	1817	1837	1847
Hull	1618	—	—	—	1711	—	—	—
Brough	1629	—	—	—	1726	—	—	—
Selby	1649	—	—	—	1749	—	—	—
Garforth	—	—	—	1803	—	—	—	1904
Leeds	1725	1751	1805	1818	1825	1851	1908	1918
New Pudsey	—	—	—	1828	—	—	—	1928
Bradford Int.	—	—	—	1838	—	—	—	1938
Halifax	—	—	—	1850	—	—	—	1950
Hebden Bridge	—	—	—	1901	—	—	—	2001
Burnley man Rd	—	—	—	1921	—	—	—	2021
Accrington	—	—	—	1931	—	—	—	2031
Blackburn	—	—	—	1939	—	—	—	2039
Preston	—	—	—	1956	—	—	—	2056
Poulton-le-Fyld	—	—	—	2014	—	—	—	2114
Blackpool North	—	—	—	2024	—	—	—	2124
Dewsbury	1737	1803	1817	—	1837	1903	—	—
Huddersfield	1747	1813	1827	—	1847	1913	1927	—
Stalybridge	1810	—	1849	—	—	—	1949	—
Manchester Picc.	1825	1855	1907	—	1923	1955	2007	—
Manchester Apt.	1858b	1910	1942b	—	1958b	2010	2041b	—
Manchester Ox Rd	1839b	1906b	1909	—	1939b	—	2009	—
Birchwood	1910e	—	1925	—	2010b	—	2025	—
Warrington Ctl	1857b	—	1930	—	1957b	—	2030	—
Liverpool L St.	1930b	—	1957	—	2029b	—	2058	—

- **a** Arrival time
- **b** Change at Manchester Piccadilly
- **d** Departure time
- **e** Change at Manchester Piccadilly and Manchester Oxford Road
- **f** Change at York
- **g** Change at Newcastle and York
- **h** Change at Durham and York
  You can reserve a seat on this train.
  There is a trolley service providing snacks, sandwiches and hot and cold drinks for all or part of the journey.

Service No. Code/Days	X61 Not Sat	X61	X61	X61	X61	X61	X64	X61	X61	X61	X61	X61	X61
MANCHESTER Chorlton St Coach Stn	—	—	—	—	—	0845	—	0945	1045	1145	1245	1345	1445
Rivington Service Station (M61)	—	—	—	—	—	0915	—	1015	1115	1215	1315	1415	1515
BOLTON Moor Ln Bus Station (Z)	—	—	—	—	—	—	1000	—	—	—	—	—	—
CHORLEY Bus Station	—	—	—	—	—	—	1030	—	—	—	—	—	—
PRESTON Bus Station arr.	—	—	—	—	—	0955	1055	1055	1155	1255	1355	1455	1555
PRESTON Bus Station (65) dep.	0600	0615	0710	0805	0900	1000	1100	1100	1200	1300	1400	1500	1600
BLACKPOOL Pleasure Beach	—	—	—	—	—	1035	1135	1135	1235	1335	1435	1535	1635
BLACKPOOL Talbot Rd Bus Stn (Y)	0630	0645	0745	0845	0945	1045	1145	1145	1245	1345	1445	1545	1645
CLEVELEYS Bus Station	0645	0700	0800	0900	1000	1100	1100	1200	1300	1400	1500	1600	1700
FLEETWOOD ——Queens Terrace	—	0715	0815	0915	1015	1115	1215	1215	1315	1415	1515	1615	1715

Airport and Flight Time	Day of Dep.	Approx. Dep. UK	Day of Rtn.	Approx Rtn. UKs	No of Nights	Travel Code
COSTA DORADA (Reus Airport)						
GATWICK 2 hrs	Tue	2345	Wed	0455	7/14	GAN20
LUTON 2 hrs	Tue	0600	Tue	1055	7/14	LAN20
STANSTED 2 hrs	Mon	1350	Mon	1850	7/14	SAN10
CARDIFF 2 hrs	Mon	0730	Mon	1220	7/14	CAN10
BIRMINGHAM 2 hrs	Mon	0800	Mon	1315	7/14	BAN10
MANCHESTER 2 hrs	Tue	2100	Wed	0430	7/14	RAN20
NEWCASTLE 2 hrs	Mon	1350	Mon	1235	7/14	NAN10
GLASGOW 2 hrs	Mon	0900	Mon	1515	7/14	AAN10

Airport and Flight Time	Day of Dep.	Approx. Dep. UK	Day of Rtn.	Approx Rtn. UKs	No of Nights	Travel Code
CYPRUS (Paphos Airport)						
BIRMINGHAM 4 hrs	Wed	1255	Wed	2315	7/14	BJG30
	Wed	0755	Wed	1810	7/14	BJG30
MANCHESTER 4 hrs	Wed	1145	Wed	2200	7/14	RJG30
	Wed	0900	Wed	1925	7/14	RGH30
GLASGOW 5 hrs	Wed	0800	Wed	1845	7/14	AJG30
	Wed	0850	Wed	2005	7/14	AJG30
TURKEY (Antalya Airport)						
GATWICK 4 hrs	Sun	2200	Mon	0655	7/14	GHD70
MANCHESTER 4 hrs	Sun	2230	Mon	0815	7/14	RHD70

1. What does the symbol 'd' mean on a train timetable?
2. Where do you need to change trains if there is a 'g' symbol on the Newcastle to Liverpool timetable?
3. Does the 06:50 from Edinburgh stop at Lockerbie?
4. What is the earliest time that I can catch a X64 bus from Bolton to Fleetwood?
5. For how long does the 08:45 X61 bus stop in Preston station?

How long do these journeys take?
1. The 15:05 train from Rugby to Watford Junction
2. The 7:55 train from Aberdeen to Crewe
3. The 14:18 train from Preston to London
4. The X64 bus from Chorley to Cleveleys
5. The 17:15 from York to Leeds

You will be using more than one timetable for these questions. How long do these journeys take?
1. From Carlisle to Blackpool Pleasure Beach if we take the 08:20 train from Carlisle to Preston, then the 10:00 bus from Preston to Blackpool Pleasure Beach?
2. From Leeds to Costa Dorada if we leave Leeds train station at 17:51, travelling to Manchester Airport to then catch the 21:00 hours flight to Costa Dorada?
3. From Edinburgh to Cyprus if we leave Edinburgh train station at 06:50 travelling to Glasgow Central, then take a taxi to Glasgow airport for the flight to Cyprus?
4. From Chorley to London if we leave Chorley by bus to catch the 12:18 train from Preston station to London?
5. From Middlesbrough to Turkey if we leave Middlesbrough train station at 17:13, travelling to Manchester Airport to then catch the flight to Turkey?

5 Measures

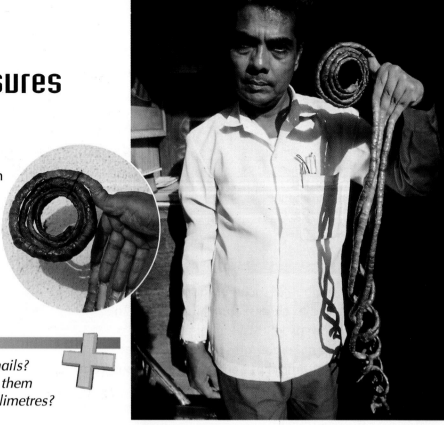

5.1 Length

The longest thumbnail in the world was 135 cm long. Why do you think anybody would want to have nails like this? How long do you think they took to grow?

- *How long are your nails?*
- *Would you measure them in centimetres or millimetres?*

We use measurements to sort things by size. The measures below are for kitchen cupboards.

❶ Sort them into a list that starts with the narrowest units.

❷ What do you notice about the height of the units?

❸ Why do you think they are designed this way?

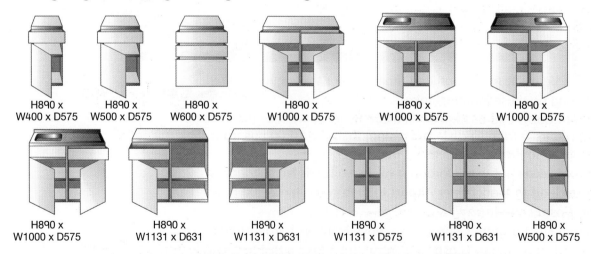

| H890 x W400 x D575 | H890 x W500 x D575 | H890 x W600 x D575 | H890 x W1000 x D575 | H890 x W1000 x D575 | H890 x W1000 x D575 |

| H890 x W1000 x D575 | H890 x W1131 x D631 | H890 x W1131 x D631 | H890 x W1131 x D575 | H890 x W1131 x D631 | H890 x W500 x D575 |

Arrange these centimetre lengths into ascending order.

❶ 23 17 64 91 36   ❺ 86 35 90 26 35

❷ 47 19 39 31 3   ❻ 49 23 19 81 62

❸ 48 64 28 97 34   ❼ 56 12 4 91 64

❹ 54 99 24 56 17   ❽ 18 11 30 96 3

Changing units

Sometimes measurements use more than one unit. This makes sorting them by size a little more difficult. Before you do anything else you must convert all the measurements to the same units.

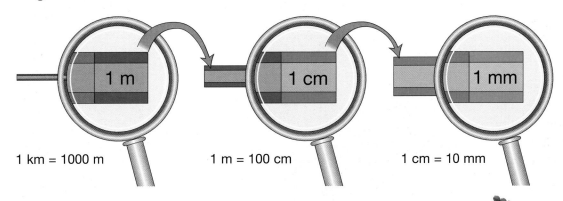

1 m	1 cm	1 mm
1 km = 1000 m	1 m = 100 cm	1 cm = 10 mm

Convert these lengths from centimetres to millimetres.

❶ 4 cm ❸ 3.7 cm ❺ 6 cm ❼ 7.8 cm
❷ 10 cm ❹ 2.5 cm ❻ 1.9 cm ❽ 12.4 cm

Convert these lengths from metres to centimetres.

❶ 3 m ❸ 1.25 m ❺ 6.05 m ❼ 7.2 m
❷ 0.8 m ❹ 4.98 m ❻ 0.12 m ❽ 6.83 m

Convert these lengths from kilometres to metres.

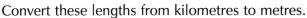

❶ 7 km ❸ 3.76 km ❺ 0.06 km ❼ 0.72 km
❷ 9.245 km ❹ 0.413 km ❻ 6.12 km ❽ 10.147 km

Arrange these lengths into ascending order.

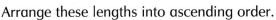

❶ 10 000 mm   100 m   1.5 km   100 000 cm   100 mm
❷ 25 cm   600 mm   3 m   250 cm   7000 mm
❸ 5 km   330 m   2900 cm   3.9 km   760 m
❹ 2400 mm   3 km   450 m   64 cm   670 mm
❺ 50 m   2450 cm   1375 mm   29.5 m   31 km

Which units would you use to measure the following?

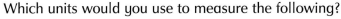

❶ The length of a football pitch
❷ The width of a human hair
❸ The distance to the school office
❹ The distance between London and New York
❺ The length of a paper clip

5.2 Mass

The largest fish in the photograph was two metres long and weighed 63.2 kilograms. Small tropical fish can be only a few centimetres long and weigh less than five grammes.

- *Do you think fishing is cruel? Why?*
- *What about keeping tropical fish? Why?*

Arrange these masses, in grammes, into ascending order.

❶ 25 45 38 16 79
❷ 39 70 12 72 54
❸ 18 98 17 32 5
❹ 87 36 64 83 27
❺ 88 45 19 8 40

❻ 21 18 6 97 2
❼ 67 43 77 12 98
❽ 52 30 41 20 16
❾ 33 26 35 48 60
❿ 19 3 88 24 39

Grammes and kilogrammes

Units of weight are based on grammes in the same way that units of length are based on metres. So, one kilogramme contains 1000 grammes.

1 kg = 1000 g

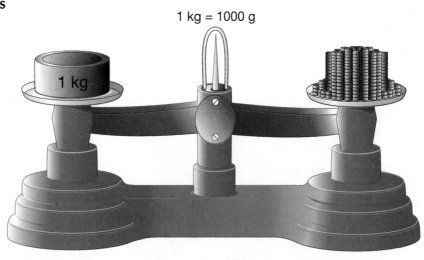

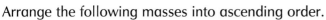

Convert the following masses from grammes to kilogrammes.

❶ 2000 g ❹ 750 g ❼ 2148 g ❿ 2234 g
❷ 6500 g ❺ 35 g ❽ 1111 g ⓫ 1948 g
❸ 1250 g ❻ 1873 g ❾ 101 g ⓬ 7091 g

Convert the following masses from kilogrammes to grammes.

❶ 4 kg ❹ 11.3 kg ❼ 9.2 kg ❿ 3.1 kg
❷ 8.5 kg ❺ 6.25 kg ❽ 7.43 kg ⓫ 5 kg
❸ 0.7 kg ❻ 1.06 kg ❾ 2.24 kg ⓬ 1.98 kg

Arrange the following masses into ascending order.

❶ 400 g 3.5 kg 6800 g 21 kg 10 kg
❷ 4.8 kg 4000 g 4.07 kg 4005 g 399 g
❸ 11 kg 1200 g 1205 g 11.65 kg 1109 g
❹ 7650 g 2453 g 2.56 kg 5.054 kg 5.4 kg
❺ 1100 g 12.6 kg 2.5 kg 2.15 kg 982 g

Which units would you use to measure the mass of the following?

❶ A new-born baby
❷ A sheet of paper
❸ A large television
❹ A small family car
❺ A professional wrestler

5.3 Capacity

Some of the barrels here hold 500 litres That is enough to fill hundreds of bottles! The barrels are stored for up to 16 years before the whiskey is ready to drink. The oldest whiskey costs the most money.

- *Why do you think whiskey is sold in small bottles?*
- *What is the biggest bottle you have ever seen?*
  What was inside it?

Millilitres and litres

The word **capacity** means the space inside something. You could measure the capacity of a bottle to see how much liquid it can hold. The capacity of a room is the space in the room. We measure the capacity of something in units based on litres.

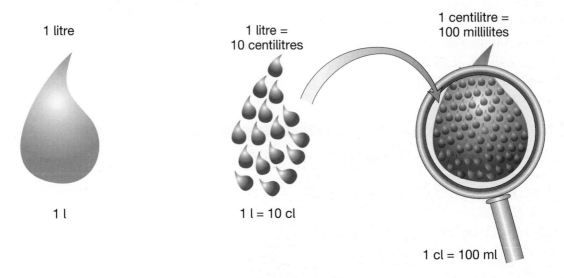

1 litre

1 l

1 litre =
10 centilitres

1 l = 10 cl

1 centilitre =
100 millilites

1 cl = 100 ml

Arrange these capacities, in centilitres, into ascending order.

❶ 125 34 250 330 19
❷ 3 279 58 167 78
❸ 632 210 98 35 100
❹ 16 3 60 98 47
❺ 21 65 20 738 38

❻ 83 27 19 134 200
❼ 60 37 4 234 590
❽ 11 88 96 91 77
❾ 52 80 104 9 376
❿ 36 86 94 110 101

Convert the following measures.

❶ 300 cl into litres
❷ 7.9 litres into ml
❸ 5200 ml into litres
❹ 3.85 litres into cl
❺ 17 cl into ml

❻ 200 ml into cl
❼ 10.6 litres into ml
❽ 1230 ml into litres
❾ 8.92 litres into cl
❿ 471 cl into litres

Arrange the following capacities into ascending order.

❶ 3 l 0.4 l 1243 ml 57.5 cl 450 ml
❷ 41.9 cl 370 cl 5.4 l 375 ml 25.6 cl
❸ 970 ml 1234 cl 157.7 cl 39.82 l 1.13 l
❹ 34 cl 92 ml 106 l 159 cl 88 ml
❺ 17 cl 81 ml 90 cl 17 ml 1.77

Which units would you use to measure the capacity of the following?

❶ A wine bottle
❷ A medicine spoon
❸ A tin of emulsion paint
❹ One bubble in a jacuzzi
❺ A large concert hall

5.4 Near enough!

The pictures on this page give you a chance to check how good you are at estimating lengths, masses and capacities. All the answers are at the back of the book. How many can you get right?

5 good
6 – 8 very good
9 – 11 excellent!
12+ did you cheat?

❶ How wide?

❷ How wide is the mouth?

❸ How long is the snake?

❹ How heavy?

❺ What is the capacity of this thermos flask?

❻ How tall?

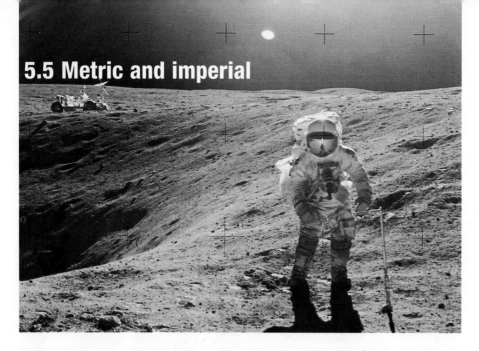

5.5 Metric and imperial

When the Americans put a man on the Moon, they measured all the distances in miles, yards, feet and inches. So the journey to the Moon was 238 906.8 miles. This is the same as 384 401 km.

- *What do you think it felt like to stand on the Moon?*
- *Would you like to go there? Why? Why not?*

In this country we measure things in a mixture of **metric** units and **imperial** units. Most countries use only metric units. The USA uses only imperial units.

Copy the table opposite into your book. Put the following quantities into the correct box in your table.
30 g   2 inches   5 lb   12 feet   5 litres   98 kg
2 pints   3 metres   10 fl oz

	Metric	Imperial
Length		
Mass		
Capacity		

Capacities

Give a rough metric equivalent for the following imperial capacities.
❶ 3 pints
❷ ½ pint
❸ 1 ½ pints
❹ 10 pints
❺ 4 ½ pints
❻ 5 pints

Lengths

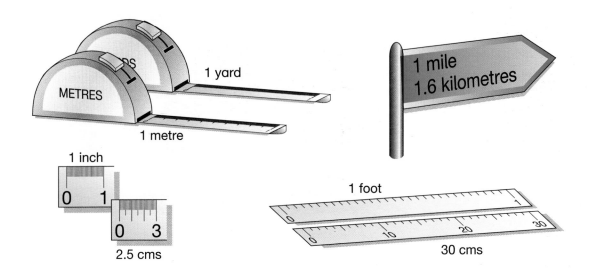

Give a rough metric equivalent for the following imperial lengths.

❶ 6 inches   ❹ 8 yards   ❼ 7 miles
❷ 3 feet   ❺ 20 inches ❽ 24 inches
❸ 10 miles   ❻ 9 feet   ❾ 6 yards

Masses

Give a rough metric equivalent for the following imperial masses.

❶ 10 lb   ❹ 6 lb   ❼ 3 lb
❷ 3 oz   ❺ 5 oz   ❽ 7 oz
❸ 2 ½ lb   ❻ 10 oz   ❾ 4 ½ lb

5.6 Days and weeks

This person changes into a werewolf on the night of the full Moon. A full Moon comes round once every four weeks. So, how many days is it safe to go round to see him? There are seven days in each week. There are 4×7 in four weeks. That makes 28 days. But, one night every four weeks he is a werewolf – that means there are $28 - 1 = 27$ safe days!

❶ How many days are there in three weeks?

❷ How many weeks are there in 56 days?

❸ How many weeks are there in 77 days?

❹ How many days are there, in total, in five weeks and three days?

❺ How many days are there, in total, in ten weeks and six days?

Hours and minutes

Dracula rises at midnight but cannot stand the daylight. If you get caught in his castle at dusk how long must you stay alive until the dawn? The Sun rises tomorrow at 6:15 am – that means you have 6 hours and 15 minutes after midnight to survive! How many minutes is that in total? Six hours each contain 60 minutes.
$6 \times 60 = 360$ minutes.
Add on the extra 15 minutes to give
$360 + 15 = 375$ minutes.

❶ How many minutes are there in two hours?

❷ How many hours are there in 660 minutes?

❸ How many minutes are there, in total, in 4 hours and 15 minutes?

❹ How many minutes are there, in total, in 6 hours and 25 minutes?

❺ How many hours are there in 420 minutes?

5.7 Reading scales

Medical staff monitor changes in their patients very carefully. A small rise in temperature may mean that the patient is developing a fever. A fever can be very dangerous so the doctors need to treat people before the illness does any serious damage.

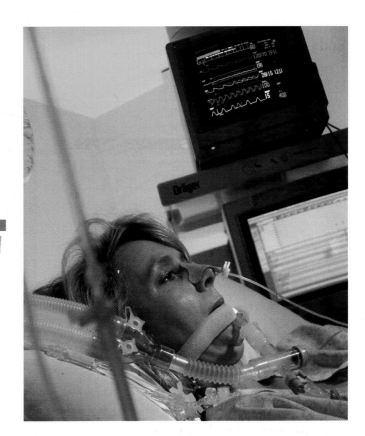

- *Have you ever had a fever? What did it feel like?*
- *Would you like to work in a hospital? Why?*

Read the temperatures on the thermometers below to one place of decimals, for example 36.5°C.

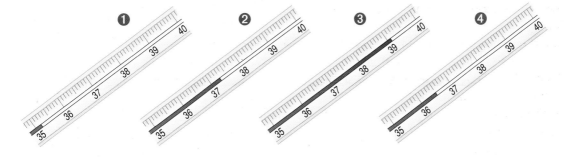

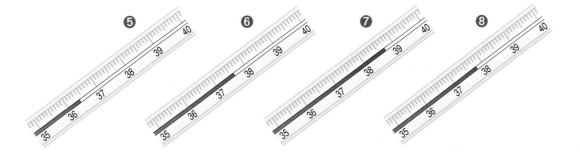

Body weight

This weighing machine gives a result to two places of decimals. So, the weight could be 47.89 kg.

Read the scales below to work out the weight of all the boxers.

①
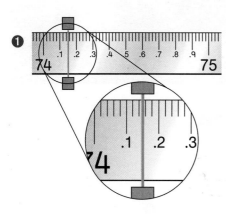

②
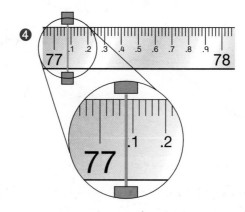

③
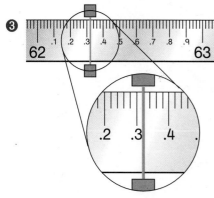

④
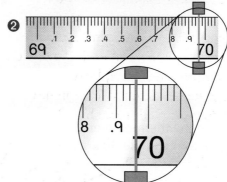

⑤
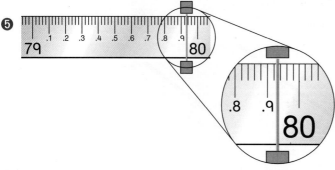

Estimates

There are many ways to measure the human body, for example, height, weight, length of arm, amount of blood. Sometimes a rough **estimate** is enough. With an estimate you aim to get near enough to the real result – don't worry about many places of decimals in your answer.

All the answers to the following questions are given in bubbles below. Try to match correct answers to the questions. The correct answers are on the back page for you to see how many you managed to get right.

❶ How long does a red blood cell live?
❷ How long is the average adult male foot?
❸ How much do you breathe in when you breathe gently?
❹ How many teeth in a full set for an adult human?
❺ How much urine do you produce every day?
❻ What is the average weight of a human brain?
❼ What is the average height of adult males in England?
❽ How long does a normal pregnancy last?
❾ What is the average life expectancy in England?
❿ How much blood does an adult male have?

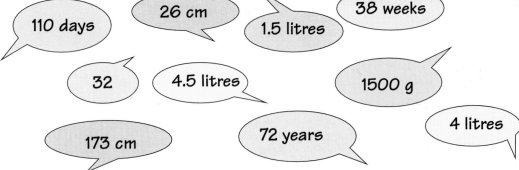

110 days   26 cm   1.5 litres   38 weeks

32   4.5 litres   1500 g

173 cm   72 years   4 litres

Estimate these measures. Then find the exact result with a suitable measuring instrument. Keep a table of data to show how close you can get.

❶ The length of this textbook
❷ The mass of this textbook
❸ The capacity of a drinking mug
❹ The capacity of a watering can
❺ The mass of a new pencil
❻ The length of an A4 sheet of paper

6 Statistics

6.1 Bar charts and tables

Every Saturday thousands of people stand in the cold to watch their heroes kick a leather ball around a field. And they pay for it!

- *Do you support a football team? Which one?*
- *What other sports would you pay to go and see?*

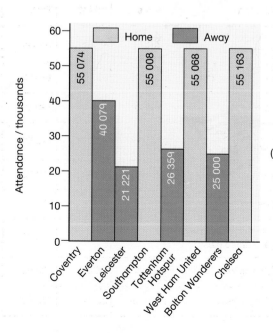

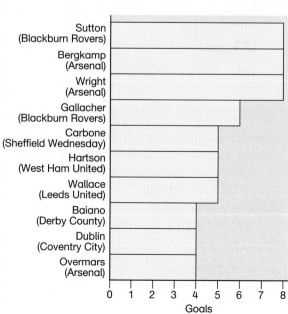

Use the bar charts on page 68 to answer these questions.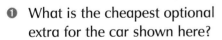

1. Which match had the largest attendance?
2. Which away match had the largest attendance?
3. What was the attendance against Chelsea?
4. Was the match against Leicester home or away?
5. How many away matches had attendances above 25 000?
6. To the nearest thousand, how many spectators do you think will fit into the Manchester United ground?

All of the questions below refer to the 1996/7 season and only include results up to the end of September.

7. How many goals has Carbone scored in the Premier League?
8. Which Blackburn Rovers player has scored twice as many Premier League goals as Overmars?
9. How many Arsenal players appear in the top ten goal scorers?
10. Which team does Wallace play for?

New wheels!

When you buy a car you can have all sorts of extras added – at a cost. What sorts of things would you buy?

1. What is the cheapest optional extra for the car shown here?
2. How much does a heated windscreen cost, excluding VAT?
3. How much VAT would you pay on alloy wheels?
4. A special offer safety pack includes a passenger airbag, power-assisted steering and fog lights for £850 including VAT. How much of a saving is this on the normal prices?
5. If you only had £200 to spend on extras what would you choose?

Options	Price £	VAT £	Total £
Airbag – front passenger	255.32	44.68	300.00
Air conditioning	421.28	73.72	495.00
Metallic paint	204.26	35.74	240.00
Power-assisted steering	353.19	61.81	415.00
Sunroof	272.34	47.66	320.00
Heated windscreen	85.11	14.89	100.00
Heated windscreen and tinted glass	153.19	26.61	180.00
Fog lights	89.36	15.64	105.00
Alloy wheels	314.89	55.11	370.00

6.2 Traffic!

It is cheaper if you pack more people in – but would you like to get into this taxi?

- *How many people are usually in the cars you travel in?*
- *Do you ever share a lift with anyone?*
- *People often don't like sharing lifts. Why do you think this is?*

Most cars have room for five people. But they are not usually full. To find out how many people travel in each car you can do a **survey**.

| Look at each car as it goes past you. | → | Note down how many people in each car. | → | Keep going until you have collected at least 20 sets of results. | → | Put your results in a tally chart. |

The train from Manchester to Liverpool was late 20 times in the last month. The chart shows how many minutes it was late each time.

3 5 7 5 3 6 9 1 4 6
7 1 5 2 7 2 9 4 2 1

Copy and complete the tally table to show the train information. The first four values have already been entered into the table.

> Every time a train is one minute late put a tally mark in this row.

Number of minutes late	Tally
1	
2	
3	I
4	
5	II
6	
7	I
8	
9	

Complete a **tally chart** for each of these lists of numbers.

❶ 7 2 3 4 2 5 4 7 4 8 6 9 3 6 3 6 1 4 5 2

❷ 120 125 123 125 123 126 127 120 121 125
123 128 129 120 124

Frequency charts

Tally charts are useful but take up a lot of space. One large survey could cover hundreds of cars but imagine the size of the chart!
A frequency table is a good summary of a tally chart.

People in car	Number of cars
1	769
2	199
3	156
4	98
5	32

This column gives the total number of tallies in each row.

A dentist counted out the number of fillings 50 of her patients had in a year. These are her results.

1 3 2 3 1 4 1 2 1 3 1 4 1 2 3 1 2 1 0 1
2 1 0 2 1 2 3 1 2 0 2 0 1 4 1 0 1 0 0 1
2 0 3 1 0 0 1 1 5 1

❶ Draw a tally chart for these results.
❷ Draw a frequency table for this information.

Draw a frequency table for each of these lists of numbers.

❶ 45 43 47 43 44 40 43 45 43 41 43 42 44
46 47 48 45 49 40 43

❷ 8.7 8.6 8.9 8.7 8.5 8.6 8.4 8.7 8.2 8.1 8.3
8.1 8.6 8.1 8.0

6.3 Pictograms

There are more cars on the roads every year. Traffic jams mean it can take hours to travel even a few miles in the city. How can anyone get to work when the roads clog up every morning?

- Campaigners say cars should be banned from cities so that people are forced to use public transport. Do you agree? Why?
- How easy is it for you to get to work every morning?

❶ How many cars were licensed in 1985?

❷ How many cars were licensed in 1990 compared with 1980?

❸ In which year were 16 million cars licensed?

❹ Which five year period shows the biggest rise in the number of cars licensed?

❺ Which five year period shows the smallest rise in the number of cars licensed?

❻ Why might it be difficult to produce a pictogram to show the *exact* number of cars licensed in a year?

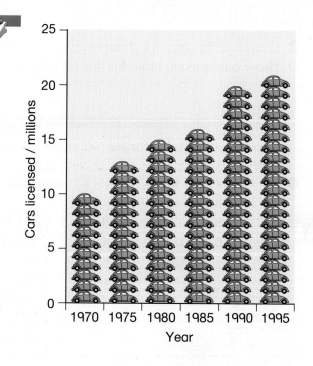

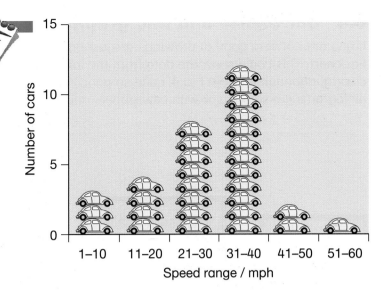

1. How many cars are there in total in this survey?
2. How many are doing less than 10 mph?
3. The speed limit in towns is 30 mph. How many cars in total were below the speed limit?
4. How many cars in total were above the speed limit?
5. How many cars were doing above 40 mph?

1. Draw a pictogram to display the results of a survey on smoking in 12 year olds.
2. Draw another pictogram to show the results for 15 year olds.
3. What differences do you notice?

Number of cigarettes smoked every day by 15 year olds	Frequency
0	25
1	5
2	10
3	10
4	5
5	15
6 or more	30

Number of cigarettes smoked every day by 12 year olds	Frequency
0	45
1	25
2	15
3	10
4	5

Two driving schools had these pass rates for their students.
1. Draw a pictogram for each driving school.
2. Which one would you go to for driving lessons? Why?

Crashless Driving School	
Pass	Frequency (%)
First try	36
Second try	56
Third try	6
Fourth try	0
Fifth try	2

Right On Driving School	
Pass	Frequency (%)
First try	44
Second try	20
Third try	14
Fourth try	8
Fifth try	14

6.4 Bar charts and line graphs

If you are not very good at drawing cars just go for a simple bar chart. This could show the data from the large traffic survey clearly, although it doesn't look quite so good. Why do you think pictograms are so popular with newspapers and magazines?

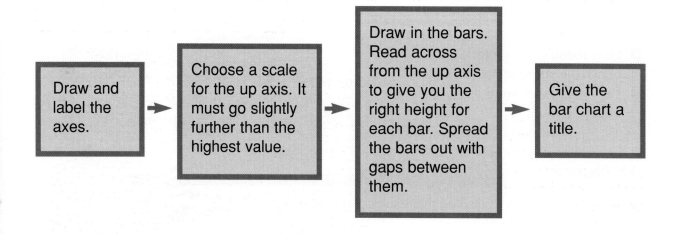

Draw and label the axes. → Choose a scale for the up axis. It must go slightly further than the highest value. → Draw in the bars. Read across from the up axis to give you the right height for each bar. Spread the bars out with gaps between them. → Give the bar chart a title.

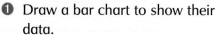

The Crighton Bank Customer Charter says that their customers should not wait more than five minutes to be served. The bank did a survey to check this promise.
❶ Draw a bar chart to show their data.
❷ Does the bank meet its customer charter's claims?

Waiting time / minutes	Number of customers
0	12
1	8
2	6
3	14
4	21
5	38
6	1

The Department of Transport publishes data about the number of accidents in different weather conditions.
❶ Draw a bar chart to show this information.

Weather conditions	Number of accidents
Snow	325
Heavy rain	550
Fog	275
Bright sunshine	325
Frost	300

A consumer magazine did a survey of the running costs of fridge freezers. The data below is a summary of their findings.

❶ Draw a bar chart they could use in their article to compare the running cost of the different brands.

Brand name	Running cost per year / £
Electrocold	52
Coldpoint	46
Zanuzzi	36
Freezone	42
Coldroom	50
Safeman	34
Burr	48

Line graphs

This iguana needs to be kept in the right conditions – not too hot or too cold. A computer records the temperature every ten minutes. It plots the results as a line graph for the keeper and switches the heater on or off.

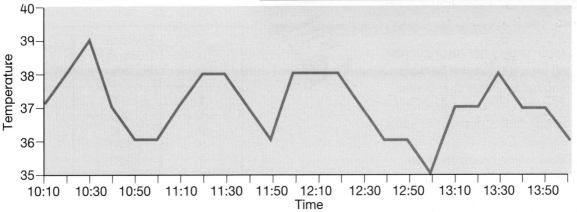

❶ Why is this chart called a line graph?
❷ What was the temperature at 11:40?
❸ What time was it when the temperature reached 39°C?

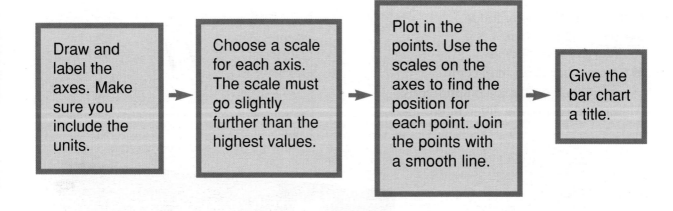

| Draw and label the axes. Make sure you include the units. | → | Choose a scale for each axis. The scale must go slightly further than the highest values. | → | Plot in the points. Use the scales on the axes to find the position for each point. Join the points with a smooth line. | → | Give the bar chart a title. |

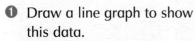

❶ Draw a line graph to show this data.

❷ I start paying into my pension fund at the age of 25. How much will I have paid in when I am 50?

❸ Use your line graph to estimate how much money I will pay in over 27 years.

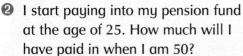

Time paying into pension fund / years	Value of contributions / £
5	15 000
10	30 000
15	45 000
20	60 000
25	75 000
30	90 000

This table shows the total interest earned by £1000 in the Benlans Building Society over five years. It also shows the average for all building societies during the same time.

❶ Draw a line graph to show how the total interest in the Benlans Building Society rose over the five years.

❷ Use the same axes to draw a graph of the average interest earned in the same time by all building societies. Label both graphs clearly so that you can tell which one is which.

Time / years	Benlans Building Society	Average interest / £
1	0	0
1	100	80
2	190	150
3	270	210
4	320	240
5	360	270

6.5 Market research

Every year big business spends thousands of pounds asking complete strangers for their opinions. They call this market research and they use it to try to find out what products people want to buy. Another set of researchers do a similar job at general elections – they ask people which way they plan to vote. Their results are used to try to predict who will form the next government.

- *Have you ever been interviewed by a market researcher? What about?*
- *How long did your interview take?*

Surveys
Think carefully before you start your survey. Good planning will make it easier to do and the results will be easier to understand. The checklist here may help.
1. How many questions will you ask?
2. What sort of answers do you expect?
3. How will you write down the answers?
4. How many people do you need to talk to?
5. How will you organise your results?

6.6 Mode and median

Why is it so difficult to get shoes that fit? And how do manufacturers know how many pairs of each size to make? And getting a style that suits can be so difficult for women with big feet.

- *Do you like shopping for shoes?*
- *How easy is it to get comfortable shoes in your size?*

Shoe shops need to know how many pairs of shoes they sell for each size. Then they know how many pairs to order from the warehouse. The data below comes from a shop in Bradford. The **mode** is the most common result. The most common shoe size for men in this country is 9 so the mode is 9.

6 3 4 7 8 3 5 6 7 7 6 9 5 7 8 8
8 6 4 5 6 7 8 6 4 5 7 8 6 7 9 6 8 7
6 4 7 9 6 5 8 7 6 7 9 5 7 6 7 10

❶ Use a tally chart to organise the data. Then draw up a frequency chart.

❷ What is the mode for the data in this sample?

Twenty-five holidaymakers were asked which airline they thought was best. These are the answers.
British Overseas; Megajet; Cityhopper; Megajet; Australian Tourist; Spanish Wings; Airbus; British Overseas; Australian Tourist; Megajet; Cityhopper; Airbus; Spanish Wings; British Overseas; Megajet; Megajet; Cityhopper; Spanish Wings; Australian Tourist; Megajet; British Overseas; Cityhopper; Australian tourist; Megajet; British Overseas.

❶ Put the results into a frequency table and find the mode.

A sports club recorded the weight of their junior players' racquets.

❶ Put the results below into a frequency table and find the modal weight.

```
319  336  313  288  315  313  319  308  342  334
315  276  328  273  319  323  288  315  308  342
316  315  336  312  276  328  273  319  315  288
```

These are the prices of 20 first aid kits on sale in a shopping centre in Leeds.

❶ Put the results into a frequency table and find the mode.

```
£18.99  £13.99  £18.99  £18.99  £14.85  £11.75  £11.75
£14.85  £17.75  £11.75  £7.99   £14.99  £13.99  £11.75
£17.75  £7.99   £11.75  £7.99   £11.75  £7.99
```

Medians

The **median** in a set of numbers is the middle number when they are put in ascending order.

1 3 4 6 8 9 15 23 27

8 is the median number in this set.

Find the median number in each of these sets of numbers.
❶ 31 2 11 42 15 17 5 24 4 27 35 7 18
❷ 197 266 232 307 299 205 198 315 202 3416 245 212
❸ 505 519 341 257 527 542 350 303 515 516 162 530
❹ 7.22 8 6.99 7.63 7 5.9 7.87 6.3 6.57 7.5 7.07 7.9 7.19

Glossary

addition	the same as 'adding', 'add together', 'find the total of' or 'find the sum of'
approximate	near to the correct answer but not exactly correct
ascending	getting bigger and bigger
bar chart	a chart using tall lengths to show quantity
capacity	the space inside something, means the same as volume
difference	the amount by which one is less than the other
deposit	money given in payment which is sometimes returnable
descending	getting smaller and smaller
division	means the same as 'share between'
equivalent	means the same as 'equal to'
estimate	the same as approximate
even	numbers which can be divided by two, for example 2, 4, 6
fraction	part of a whole number
imperial	a measuring system using inches, ounces and pints
median	the middle number in a set of ascending numbers
metric	a measuring system used by most countries
mode	the biggest group in a frequency chart
multiplication	the same as 'times' or 'find the product of'
odd	numbers that cannot be divided by two without leaving a remainder, for example 1, 3, 5
pictogram	a chart using pictures to represent quantity
place value	the position of a number
subtraction	means the same as 'take away' or 'find the difference between'
tally chart	a chart using little marks to show quantity
value	the meaning of a number
volume	the space something takes up, means the same as capacity

Answers to selected questions

2.7 Constant function addition

The word 'the' appears 41 times on pages 30 and 31. That means you would get £205.

5.4 Near enough!

1. 12 mm
2. 35 cm
3. 4 m
4. 165 kg
5. 1 litre
6. 5'8½" (174 cm)
7. 2 litres
8. 46 cm
9. 1 pint
10. 78 kg
11. 2 lbs (1 kg)
12. 120 ml
13. 90 cm
14. 7'6" (229 cm)
15. 17 g

5.7 Reading scales
Exercise 3

1. 110 days
2. 26 cm
3. 1.5 litres
4. 32
5. 4 litres
6. 1500 g
7. 173 cm
8. 38 weeks
9. 76 years
10. 4.5 litres